How To Make Your Own Fishing Lures

By Vlad Evanoff

SUNVILLAGE
publications

www.sunvillagepublications.com

How To Make Your Own Fishing Lures
By Vlad Evanoff

SUNVILLAGE
publications

Cover photography by William Berry
Cover design by www.WebCopyAlchemy.com

Preface

One of the most satisfying experiences a fisherman can have is to catch a fish on a fishing lure he has fashioned with his own hands. The trout angler has excellent books on how to tie his own flies, but little printed information has been available to anglers who want to make their own plugs, spoons, spinners, metal squids, jigs, and other fresh-and-salt-water lures. So that is how this book came to be written.

As these pages will demonstrate, it is not necessary to be a skilled craftsman to make lures. Most anglers already possess the ability to handle the few necessary tools, and if they follow the directions and also let the illustrations guide them, they can make excellent lures. The lures may not look professionally perfect, but they will catch fish, and that's all that really counts.

And if the angler makes his own lures, he'll probably catch more fish, in the long run. The reason for this is psychological. An angler who uses a store-bought plug or jig tends to be hesitant about casting it around rocks, logs, piles, and masses of seaweed. He figures he paid good money for it and doesn't want to lose it—even though he knows some of the best fish are caught around such obstructions. And other lures such as jigs are most effective when bounced on the bottom, when they often get fouled and lost. So, rather than lose his costly lures our cautious angler casts into safer spots, which contain fewer fish!

The angler who makes his own lures just doesn't have such inhibitions. He figures the lure he ties to his line cost him very little in cold cash and was fun to make. So what, if it is lost? He casts into all kinds of risky spots and loses some lures. He also catches more than his share of fish. Another good argument is that the angler who buys his lures in a store usually carries only one or two of a certain type or size. If he loses them, he's through fishing for the day, if the fish happen to want that particular lure. But the make-them-yourself angler usually has plenty of spares and rarely runs short.

Making fishing lures can be an enjoyable hobby, especially during the long winter months when fishing is slow. It has even been argued that the joy of designing and creating a lure offers as much if not more pleasure than the actual fishing.

So, have fun! Good luck and good fishing.

VLAD EVANOFF

Brooklyn, N. Y.

Contents

1

Tools

Before you can make any kind of fishing lures you must have the proper tools. In fact, without the right tools you can't do a good job, and you'll soon become discouraged. On the other hand, if you are equipped with the right tools you'll find lure-making easy and highly enjoyable. So the best procedure is to obtain as many of the necessary tools in advance before you start making your own lures.

Most anglers will already have some of the tools described here. The rest can be bought without too much of an investment, and the others can be acquired as the need arises for them. Unless you want to make all the lures in this book, you won't need every single tool listed here. If you read the chapter on the particular lure or lures you want to make, you'll get a good idea of the tools you'll need. Then make a list of the tools which will be needed to make those lures. Naturally, many of the same tools will be used for most of the fishing lures. But some lures will require special tools which must be bought or obtained.

The biggest single item needed for making fishing lures is a bench, table, or desk. Fortunate, indeed, is the man who has a basement, den, or special room where he can have a permanent workbench and various power tools to pursue his hobbies. For many this is out of the question, and they have to do their work on a kitchen table or desk which must also serve for other uses. This tends to discourage many who are irked by the chore of taking out and putting away tools and materials every time they want to work on fishing lures. If you have no permanent workbench the best solution is to keep your tools and lure-making materials in a chest, cabinet, or drawer where they are available quickly.

After you have such a bench, table, or desk you need a vise (Fig. A) which will hold the various lures for drilling, filing, bending, and other operations. Almost any bench vise of good size will serve the purpose. Unless you have a permanent workbench, this vise doesn't have to be fastened to the table or desk until needed.

A small anvil is also useful if you plan to make many metal lures or parts for such lures. It is used for cutting, bending, punching, and riveting. However, if you get a big bench vise of the machinist's or utility type you can use the anvil surface found on such vises. Or you can use a small block of iron with a smooth surface as a makeshift anvil.

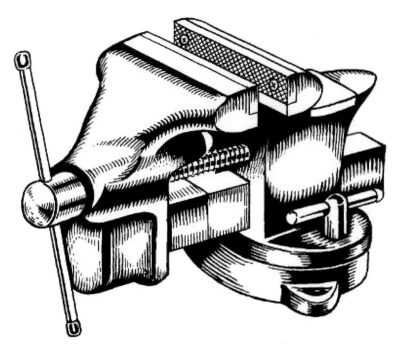

Figure A.   *Bench vise.*

A hammer, of course, is a basic tool for any kind of work, and for making fishing lures about two or three hammers will suffice. If you already have a claw hammer (Fig. B), you can use it for many lure-making jobs.   How-

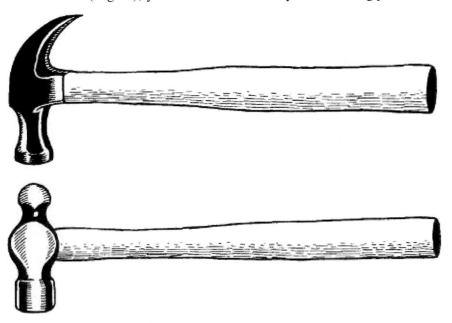

Figure B.   *Claw hammer (above) and ball peen hammer.*

Wooden mallet.   *Figure C.*

ever, you should also get at least one ball peen or machinist's hammer which can be used for shaping metal, driving punches, cold chisels, and other uses. A 12-ounce ball peen hammer is a good size for all-round work. Another type of hammer which is good to have is a soft-faced hammer. These are made of plastic or have rawhide, fiber or lead faces. The soft-faced hammer is used for bending and shaping metal and leaves no tool marks. A wooden mallet (Fig. C) is also needed if you plan to shape your own metal spoons or spinners.

At least two saws will be needed. If you already have a hand saw (Fig. D), it can be used for working with wood. Since most lures are small, however, a back saw which has a thin blade and fine teeth is even better than a large hand saw with coarse teeth for accurate cutting. The other saw which

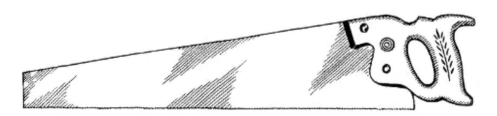

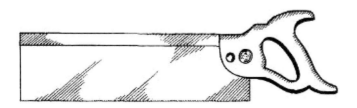

Hand saw (above) and back saw.   *Figure D.*

Figure E.

Hacksaw.

is needed is a hacksaw (Fig. E) that is used for cutting metal and other hard materials such as plastics. There are many types of hacksaws on the market, but the adjustable frame with a pistol grip is best. You will also need several kinds of blades to use with the hacksaw. These blades have from 14 to 32 teeth to the inch and come in all-hard or flexible tempers. Each type is best for a certain job, depending on the metal or material you are cutting. If you have one or two blades of each kind you'll be prepared for any cutting job. Some kind of drill is needed for drilling holes in wood and metal. If you have a home workshop with a drill press you can use it for most of the work to be done. It is especially useful when drilling holes in metal. A portable electric drill (Fig. F) is also a big aid when drilling metal, especially if you have to drill many holes. However, when making fishing lures most drilling is done in wood or softer metals such as brass and copper. Here an ordinary

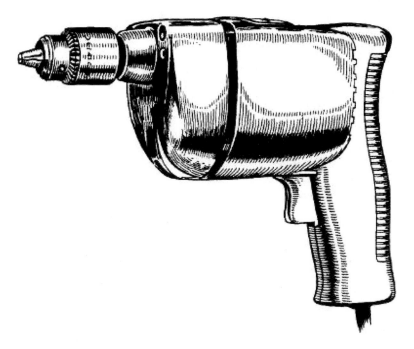

Figure F.

Portable electric drill.

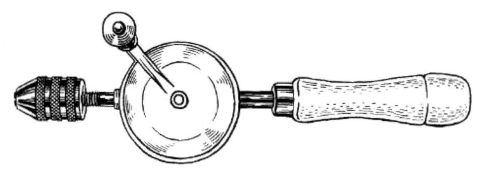

Hand drill. *Figure G.*

hand drill (Fig. G) will serve the purpose. Such a hand drill will usually take drills up to V4 in. in diameter. When buying a hand drill it's a good idea to get the best you can get. A cheap hand drill may not work properly or will soon break or wear out.

You also need a set of twist drills to use with an electric or hand drill. For the drill press or electric drill- you will need a set of high-speed drills. The high-speed drills can be used for fast drilling without losing their temper. For drilling wood or soft metals, carbon drills which are cheaper than high speed drills can be used. You should get a complete set of drills up to about 1/4 in. in diameter. The smaller sizes are the ones you will use most often. It's a good idea to buy two or three twist drills of the same size in the smaller sizes so that if you break one you'll have a spare.

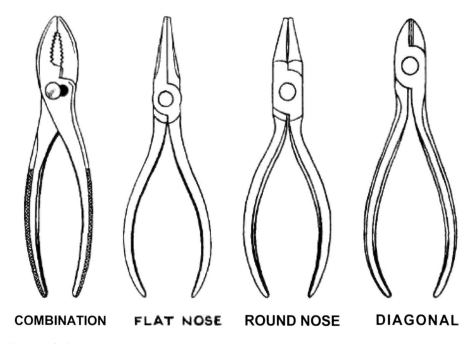

COMBINATION **FLAT NOSE** **ROUND NOSE** **DIAGONAL**

Types of pliers. *Figure H.*

A set of different kinds of pliers (Fig. H) is needed for many jobs encountered in making fishing lures. Combination pliers which have a slip joint which permits the jaws to open wide at the hinge to grip large diameters are useful for holding and bending metal.

Flat-nose pliers are also useful for holding or bending thin sheet metal or wire. They have a flat gripping surface between the jaws which will hold thin metal or wire firmly without damaging it too much.

Round-nosed pliers are needed for bending wire into various curves and eyes. They are especially useful in making spinner shafts and wire leaders. Both jaws of these pliers are round and tapered toward the end. Curves or eyes of small radius are bent with the tips of the jaws, while those of greater radius are bent with the base of the jaws. Even so, you'll need two pairs of round-nosed pliers to handle most of the work. One pair can be the regular size used for heavy work, while the other pair should be the smaller jeweler size round-nosed pliers. These are used for making very small curves or eyes and for fine wire.

Diagonal cutting pliers are used for cutting fine wire, nails, pins, and screws. The angle of the jaws on these pliers makes it possible to cut close to a surface. These pliers are designed for cutting mostly the softer metals and wire. However, they can be used for steel piano wire or stainless steel wire if they have very hard cutting jaws. Because of this you should buy the best

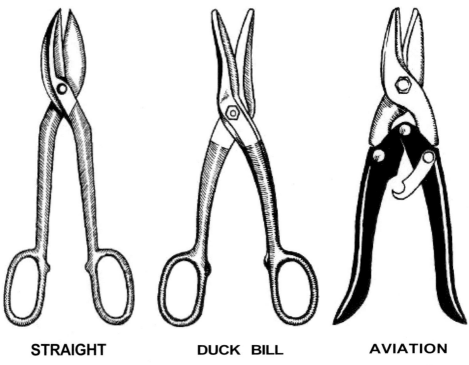

STRAIGHT   **DUCK BILL**   **AVIATION**

Figure I.   *Hand snips.*

diagonal pliers you can get. Cheap ones will not do a good cutting job, and the edges of the jaws will soon be nicked and ruined if used on hard wire.

For cutting sheet metal into various shapes you'll need hand snips (Fig. I). Although a pair of straight snips can be used both for straight cutting and for large curves, duck bill snips are more suitable for all-round work. The duck bill snips will cut straight lines or curves in either direction. These snips do not provide too much leverage, and cutting thick metal is hard work. If you want to make it easier, you can get aviation metal snips which have a compound lever action. They will cut thicker metal with much less effort.

You will also need an assortment of files to use on wood and metal. Files can be used to shape wooden fishing lures; for finishing metal molds, jigs, and other lures, for cutting tempered steel wire, hooks, metal hardware; and for finishing metal lips, propellers, spinners, and spoons. Files are also needed to keep other tools sharp and in proper working order.

There are many different types of files in use but four will take care of most of your needs (Fig. J). The flat file is one of the fastest cutting general purpose files you can use. It has a broad surface and removes wood or metal quickly. You should get three flat files with different cuts. One should be a fine single cut which is used when a smooth finish is required. Another flat file should be a double cut type which is used for removing wood or metal at a fast rate. This file leaves a rough surface which must be finished with a smooth file. The other type of flat file should be a rasp which is used for rough work when you want to remove a lot of wood.

Still another file you need is a half-round file which is also a good general purpose tool. It has a flat face for flat filing and a curved side for filing curves. This file can also be obtained in different grades of coarseness.

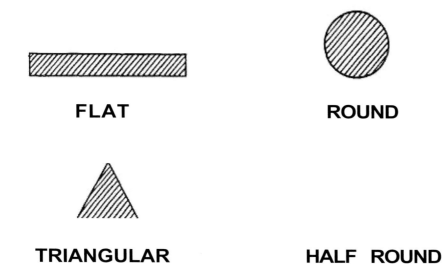

FLAT   **ROUND**

TRIANGULAR   **HALF ROUND**

Shapes of files.   *Figure J.*

A triangular or three-square file is used for filing metal smooth where small surfaces or corners must be worked. It can also be used to cut through heavy wire, rods, fishhooks, and other metal which cannot be cut with ordinary pliers. The triangular file is also handy for sharpening chisels, knives, and other cutting edges.

The round file or "rattail" file, as the name implies, is round and tapered toward the end. It is used to enlarge holes and for filing small half-round curves.

You'll also need an assortment of screw drivers of various lengths and blades. The standard screw driver with a handle, shank, and blade will be the one mostly used and should be obtained in the smaller sizes. You rarely use big screws when making fishing lures, so smaller screw drivers will be used most of the time.

The screws used in making lures are either plain or nickel-plated round-head brass screws. The sizes mostly used are No. 1 by 3/8 in., No. 2 by 3/8 in., No. 2 by 1/2 in., and No. 2 by 5/8 in. They should be brass because iron screws rust and weaken the wood, then pull out.

An electric soldering iron will be required for some jobs. Soldering irons come in Various sizes, but the 90- or 100-watt iron is a good general purpose type (Fig. K). With this, of course, you'll need soft solders which are alloys of lead and tin. They can be obtained in wire, ribbon, or bar form. The wire solder is the most convenient since it has a hollow core like a tube which contains a flux. If you use bar solder you'll have to buy a flux such as rosin or soldering paste. This is used to remove the oxide coating from metals so that the solder will take.

Figure K.   *Electric soldering iron.*

Then we have various punches, used for different purposes when making fishing lures (Fig. L). The most useful is the center punch which is used to make a mark showing where to drill. For drilling wood you can, of course, use an ordinary ice pick or awl to make a starting hole. But for metal you need the center punch which is struck with a hammer to make such an indentation. These punches come in various diameters and tapers, and two or three sizes will handle most jobs. Another handy punch is a starting punch which has a long gradual taper and a blunt point. This is used for clearing holes and can also be used to open the eyes on big hooks.

You should also possess at least one flat, cold chisel, which is used for cutting sheet metal, lead, tin, and other metals where other cutting tools cannot be used.

Center punch (above) and starting punch.   *Figure L.*

Finally, you'll need a sharp knife, single-edge razor blade, scissors, dividers, calipers, and a metal rule.

If you really plan to go into making wooden plugs seriously you'll find a wood or metal turning lathe invaluable for turning down such lures. Of course, this is quite an investment, and unless you really plan to make many fishing plugs, it doesn't pay to buy a lathe especially for this purpose. But if you already have one you can use it for such work.

Somewhat less expensive but very handy is one of those hobby motorized tools which hold a large variety of small rotary tools. It can be used for drilling, grinding, polishing, and carving. This tool is especially useful for finishing off metal molds.

When whittling or shaping wooden plugs or other lures by hand you find a set of wood-carving tools very useful. These have small chisel type blades which can be used to cut grooves, cups, holes, and similar indentations. The gouges which are part of these tools are especially useful for this work.

Then there are various materials such as wood, metal, paints, lacquers, varnishes, hooks, screw eyes, wire, and other fishing lure parts which you will need. These will be described in the following chapters in detail, as the need arises for them. They can usually be bought in hardware stores, fishing tackle stores, or mail-order houses. Mail-order houses often carry a large stock of fishing lure parts. Write for their catalogs to get descriptions of the lure parts with prices.

Fresh-Water Plugs

The lure known as a "plug" had its origins in the distant past, and no one is sure who made the first lure for fresh-water fishing. The modern wooden fishing plug had its beginnings around 1900, and in the following years several companies started to manufacture these lures for black bass. Later they made larger and stronger plugs for pike, muskellunge, and salmon.

Plugs are now widely used in fresh-water fishing, as a look at any fishing tackle store showcase or counter will reveal. Today there are many different types, sizes, shapes, and colors of plugs on the market. The angler who wants to make his own plugs can duplicate many of the more popular models. However, there are a few basic types, and the construction of these will be covered in this chapter.

To make plugs you will need wood which can be cut into small blocks and then shaped to the size and form you require. The best all-round wood for making fishing plugs is cedar. Straight-grained white cedar is excellent since it is light, strong, and easy to work. It also stands up better in the water than most woods. Red cedar can also be used instead of the white variety. Other woods which can be used for making plugs are basswood and birch.

Most of these woods can be obtained at a lumber yard in large blocks or round logs. They can then be sawed with a circular saw or hand saw into convenient small blocks about 6 in. long and about IV2 in. square.

The fastest way to shape wooden plugs is with a lathe. With a wood-turning lathe or even a metal-turning lathe, for that matter, you can shape the plugs quickly and uniformly in fairly large quantities. If you already have such a lathe, so much the better.

When turning down plugs with a lathe, mount one of the wooden blocks between the centers. Measure and mark the length of the plug you are making on the wood block with a pencil so you know where both ends will fall. Then start the lathe and, using the wood-turning tools, shape the wood to the correct diameter, taper, and shape of the model you are copying. After this is done take some sandpaper and sand the plug very smooth as it is turning. Then cut the finished plug off from the rest of the wood.

If you have no lathe you can turn out plugs at a fair speed with ordinary hand tools. You can whittle plugs from the softer woods with an ordinary sharp knife if you prefer to work that way. However, a somewhat easier and quicker method is to secure the block of wood in a bench vise and then use a rasp to take off the corners. If you cut the block of wood almost the diameter of the finished plug, you will have less filing to do. In other words, if the finished plug will be an inch in diameter, start with a block of wood of about the same diameter or a bit more. Then you only have to round off the corners with the rasp. After using the rasp for the rough work finish shaping the plug with a wood file. Then it can be made smooth by using different grades of sandpaper.

Several basic body shapes are used in making fresh-water plugs. An old-time favorite is the "wobbler" type shown in Fig. 1. This plug is simple to make since it is uniform in thickness with a rounded tail and a grooved head. It should be about 3 3/4 in. long and 3/4 in. in diameter. The dimensions given for all the wooden plugs here are the so-called "bait-casting" size. These are fairly large fresh-water plugs suitable for use with bait-casting, spin casting, or spinning rods. They weigh about 5/8 of an ounce when finished. If you want smaller plugs strictly for use with light spinning tackle, make them about one third smaller than the dimensions given here.

A simple way to make the wobbler type plug is to cut the head at a 45-degree angle, as shown in Fig. 2. However most of these plugs are made with a grooved head. To do this, cut the plug at the same angle, then carve out the head with a rotary file mounted in a drill press or hand motor tool. If you haven't got such power tools, use a small gouge to cut out the groove.

To complete the wobbler plug you'll need three treble hooks and four screw eyes. To start the screw eye in the wood, first take an ice pick or awl and push it into the wood where the screw eyes will go to make small holes. Then put the screw eyes into the holes and twist them in. The screw eye which goes at the head of the plug (where the fishing line is tied) is forced in "as is." Pliers can be used to screw it in. The other three screw eyes hold hooks and if the screw eyes are closed they must be opened. Then slip a treble hook over the eye and close it. If you want to give the plug a professional look, slip small disc or cup washers over the shank of the screw eye before you force then into the plug (see Fig. 3). Two treble hooks are attached below the plug and the third at the rear or tail.

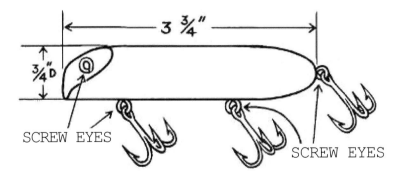

Wobbler plug.   *Figure 1.*

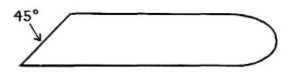

Figure 2.   *Simple wobbler plug with 45° angle head.*

Screw eyes make inexpensive simple hook hangers and are strong enough for most fresh-water plugs. However, you can also use special hook hangers to attach the treble hooks. These are small metal saddles with a stop that prevents a hook from fouling with other hooks or the fishing line on a cast, or when the lure strikes the water. The hook hangers have two small holes on each end and are attached to the plug with small screws, as shown in Fig. 4.

Next we have the surface plugs which ride on top of the water and create some kind of commotion, such as a splash or ripple. One of the simplest of these is the "popper" type. It is easy to make a popping plug, using the same plug body as the wobbler plug described above. You simply turn the plug around and attach the hooks on the opposite side, as shown in Fig. 5. Here

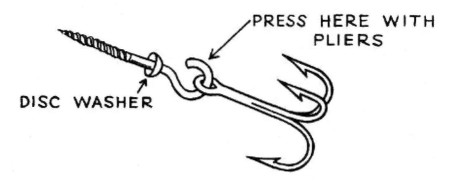

Figure 3.   *Treble hook on screw eye.*

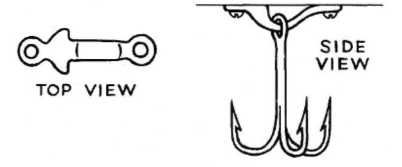

Figure 4.   *Hook hanger.*

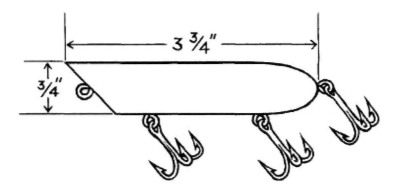

Popping plug with three treble hooks.   *Figure 5.*

you do not necessarily need a grooved head. A head cut at a 45° angle will
provide plenty of splash and commotion when jerked. This plug is also made
with three treble hooks. However, if you are making a smaller version of this
plug for use with spinning tackle, it can have only two trebles—one at the
belly and the other at the tail.

The typical popping type of surface plug is shown in Fig. 6. This plug
has a wide, cupped head and then tapers to a narrow tail. It should be about
2 3/4 in. long with the head section 1 1/8 in. in diameter and tapering to a
tail about ⅝ in. thick. This lure has one screw eye at the head in the center
of the cupped head and two treble hooks, one at the belly and the other at
the tail. Because of its shape, this popping plug is most easily made when
turned down on a lathe. However if you don't mind the work involved,
whittle or file it down with hand tools.

Another type of surface plug which was popular many years ago and is
still a good fish getter is the "collar" type shown in Fig. 7. It is easily turned
down on a lathe in a short time. Make it about 3 in. long and 3/4 in. in diameter, the collar extending about 1/4 in. from the rest of the body.
Since

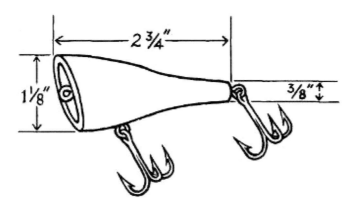

Another typical popping plug.   *Figure 6.*

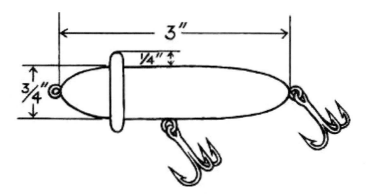

Figure 7.   *Collar type plug.*

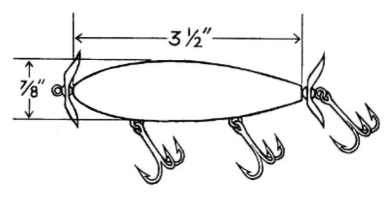

Figure 8.   *Propeller type surface plug.*

this collar encircles the plug it makes a foolproof splasher, no matter how it lands in the water. When jerked it will throw a spray which attracts fish. This plug has one screw eye at the head or nose and two treble hooks, one at the belly and the other at the tail.

Another surface plug which has proven effective over the years is the "propeller" type, Fig. 8. This plug has one or two propellers, usually one at the head and another at the tail. When it is retrieved or jerked the propeller blades revolve and throw a spray. Although screw eyes can be used to hold the propeller blades, a much better and stronger method is to rig this plug with a wire running through the center, as shown in Fig. 9. When making

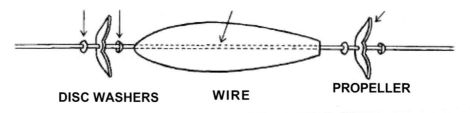

DISC WASHERS   **WIRE**   **PROPELLER**

Figure 9.   *Assembly of propeller plug.*

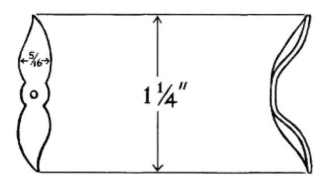

Shape and size of propeller.   *Figure 10.*

this plug, drill a hole through the center, from the head to the tail. If you have a drill press, do this with an extra long drill and a jig which will hold the plug body in the correct position. You can also drill such a hole very easily with a hand drill—if you do it before the plug is shaped. In other words, drill the hole in the rectangular block of wood through the center, then rasp and file to finish the plug. To find the center of the block of wood, draw an X from corner to corner.

The propellers for this plug can be cut out of sheet brass, as shown in Fig. 10. You can do some of the cutting with hand snips, then use flat and triangular files to finish the job. A hole must then be drilled in the propeller. Finally, twist the blades in opposite directions and slant them back so they will spin.

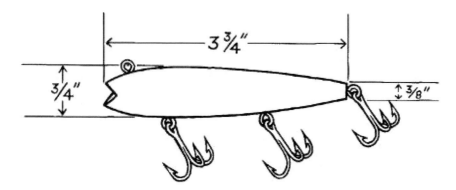

Darter type plug.   *Figure 11.*

To assemble this plug you need some wire such as the heavier gauges of stainless steel wire. Cut a short length of about 7 or 8 in. Then, using the round-nosed pliers, form an eye on one end (instructions for doing this can be found in Chap. 12). But before you complete the eye, slip on a treble hook. Then slip on a washer, which will act as a bearing for the propeller blade. This can be a disc or cup washer, a grommet or a bead, whichever is handy. Next, slip on the propeller blade, add another washer, and run the wire through the wood plug body from the rear or tail. Slip on another washer, then the second propeller blade, and finally the remaining washer. Now form the second eye in front, to which the line will be attached. To complete the plug, screw in another treble hook at the belly.

Another effective plug is the "darter" type shown in Fig. 11. This plug is 3% in. long with a head about ^3A in. in diameter and tapers to a tail ^{3}/s in. thick. The head slopes downward, starting about one inch from the end.

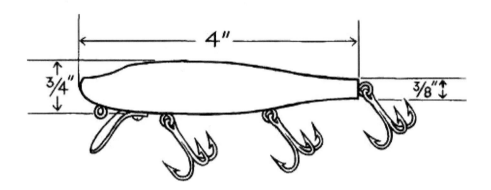

Figure 12.   *Underwater plug.*

Then a small notch is cut or filed at the nose of the plug. This plug also has three treble hooks attached, two at the belly and one at the tail. The screw eye for holding the fishing line is screwed in at the top of the head where it slopes.

The strictly "underwater" plug shown in Fig. 12 is an old-time favorite that has taken fresh-water fish consistently through the years. The large

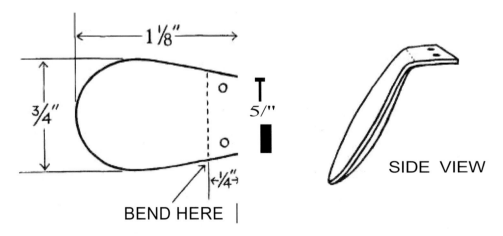

Figure 13.   *Metal lip for underwater plug.*

bait-casting size in this plug consists of a body about 4 in. long, 3/4 in. in diameter, and the tail tapers to 3/8 of an inch. The head part is round with a
concave cut on top. This can easily be done with a half-round file or by
holding the plug against a revolving grindstone.

The underwater plug requires a metal lip which makes it dive, wriggle,
and travel under the surface. The shape and dimensions of this lip are shown
in Fig. 13. It can be cut out from sheet brass, and two holes are drilled to
take small screws for fastening the lip to the wood body. Although a straight
metal lip will give the plug some action, better results are obtained if the lip
is bent like a shallow plate or saucer. This can be done by hammering the
metal lip gently with a ball peen hammer. The hammering can be done
against a block of hard wood which has a depression gouged out to take the
metal lip.

When assembling the underwater plug, start by screwing in a screw eye
under the head to which the line will be attached. Then fasten on the metal
lip with two small screws just behind this screw eye. Next, about an inch behind the metal lip, screw in one of the treble hooks. A second treble hook is
attached about mid way between the first one and the tail, and the final
treble hook is attached to the tail.

The "jointed" plug is easily made by using the same body as the underwater plug described above. Only here you cut the wood body in half, as
shown in Fig. 14. The two parts are then connected by screw eyes. The rest
of the plug is assembled the same way as the underwater type, except that
only two instead of three treble hooks are used.

As mentioned before, the dimensions given here are for the larger bait-
casting size. These plugs will run from about 1/2 to 3/4 ounces in weight. You
don't have to follow the dimensions given here; make the plugs smaller if
you want to! The small spinning-size plugs can be made one-third smaller
and these will weigh between 1/4 and 1/2 oz.

The treble hooks used on the larger bait-casting size plugs should be

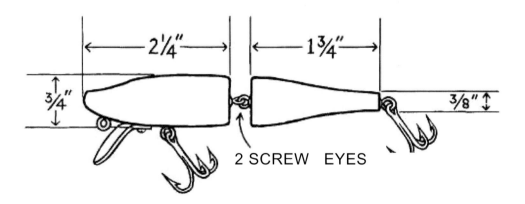

Jointed underwater plug.   *Figure 14.*

either sizes No. 1 or 1 /0. For the smaller spinning size, plugs No. 2 or 4 are more suitable. Such hooks can be bought in fishing tackle stores, of order them by mail.

If you haven't got the time or desire to turn out the plug bodies with hand tools you can order different types and sizes of finished wood bodies from some of the mail-order houses. These wooden bodies are already shaped and sanded smooth so that all you have to do is assemble the parts, such as the hardware and hooks. If you want to make plastic plugs, order such bodies

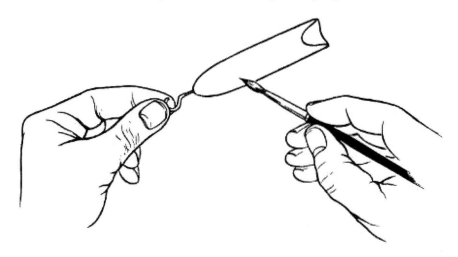

Figure 15.   Screw eye or hook for holding plug body while it is being painted, sprayed, or dipped.

from the mail-order houses. Some of these plastic plugs come complete, all ready for adding the hooks and other metal parts. Others come in two sections and must be cemented together.

Before making the wooden plugs described above, decide how they will be painted. If you plan to dip the plug bodies in enamel or lacquer or spray them with an airbrush, this should be done before they are assembled. If you plan to paint them with a small brush, assemble the plugs first and paint them later.

If several wood bodies are to be painted at the same time, you'll find the quickest method is to dip them into a can of white lacquer or enamel. Before you do this, screw in a small screw eye or hook into the tail for holding while dipping and hanging while drying. See Fig. 15. For best results, the lacquer or enamel should be fairly thin and after the plug body is dipped once it should be allowed to dry, then dipped again, as many times as is necessary for a good, thick coat. Usually this base coat will take three or four dippings.

You can also spray on solid colors such as white or silver with an airbrush, or by using one of those pressurized paint cans which can be bought in al-

MASKING TAPE

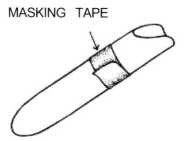

Tape around a plug, when painting or spraying a red head. *Figure 16.*

most any hardware store. These are handy to use and the colors dry fast.

If you paint the wood bodies by hand with a brush, you'll find enamel is best. It can be applied fairly thick and usually two coats of white will do the job.

After you have applied the white base coat and it is dry, you are ready to apply other colors. A simple way to make a red-and-white plug is to use a strip of masking tape all around the plug about an inch from the nose. See Fig. 16. Then spray or paint the head part with bright red. When it dries you can remove the masking tape and you'll have a clean, sharp dividing line between the red and white.

Another good color combination for fresh-water plugs is a lure with a light blue or green back and silver sides. This looks like many of the minnows found in fresh-water rivers and lakes. To apply these colors, start with an all-white plug and brush on light blue or green enamel. When the color is still wet, brush on silver or aluminum paint along both sides of the plug. Where the silver meets the light blue or green, blend colors until they are well mixed.

To make a natural fish scale finish on a wood plug, spray blue, green, or brown over the top or back and sides of the basic white-coated body. Leave the belly of the plug white. When this dries use a cloth netting tacked loosely on a wooden frame to apply the scale finish. Hold the plug against this netting from the opposite side while you spray on the silver with an artist's air

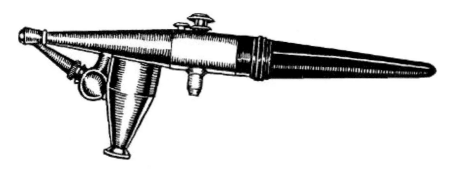

Artist airbrush. *Figure 17.*

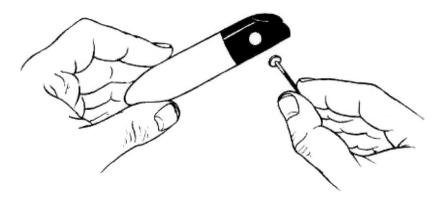

Figure 18.   *Using a flat-head nail to paint eyes on a plug.*

brush. To get the best results you need an artist's airbrush such as the Paasche type (Fig. 17). With the airbrush you'll need a tank of compressed air or a compressor motor. The artist's type airbrush results in fine work and you get the best results with it when making scale finishes or other patterns. With such an airbrush, also, you can work out various color combinations on your plugs and give them a real professional look. But if you have no airbrush, don't despair—with a little practice you can do a pretty good paint job with a brush.

After the plugs are painted you may wish to give them a more complete look by adding eyes, although eyes are not necessary to catch fish. Most store-bought plugs have glass eyes. These are similar to the eyes used by taxidermists and can be obtained from them. They are mounted on wire which is clipped off with cutting pliers, leaving a short length of wire of-about V^* in. long. Then drill holes in the plug, put in some quick-drying cement, and insert the glass eyes into the holes. You can also paint the eyes with a small, pointed brush or dab them on with a flat head nail dipped in yellow paint. After the yellow dries use a smaller flat head nail dipped in black to apply the pupil of the eye. See Fig. 18.

The fishing plugs described above and suggestions for making them are just a starter for the ambitious "do-it-yourself angler. Many different kinds of plug can be made or created. The angler can experiment with plug weights and shapes and work out a lure most suitable for the waters he fishes. One angler may want big, strong plugs to use for such large fish as muskellunge, pike, Pacific salmon, etc. Naturally, he will use larger plug bodies, stronger, heavier hooks and heavy hardware and fittings. Another angler may want small, light lures to use for such small fish as trout, bass, and panfish. He will make much smaller plugs and use lighter hooks and hardware. Still another angler may want to create a plug which resembles some particular minnow or small animal which fish feed on in the waters he fishes.

All of these anglers can usually meet such demands more exactly by making or designing their own fishing plugs.

3

Fresh-Water Spin Bugs

One of the most effective lures for black bass in fresh water is the so-called "bass bug" which is used with a fly rod. However, these bugs are too light to cast with a casting or spinning rod. But the angler who wants to use such tackle can easily make bass bugs which are heavy enough to cast.

Such lures (which I will call "spin bugs" to separate them from the regular cork or plastic "bass bugs") should weight at least 1/4 oz. or a bit more to cast well. They are usually bulky, having hair or feathers which hold them back during the cast.

Spin bugs or bass bugs are usually made to resemble some kind of insect or bug which has fallen into the water. These are generally such big insects as dragonflies, butterflies, moths, beetles, and grasshoppers. Such insects float and kick around on top of the water, so spin bugs which do the same are the best fish-getters. However, some of these lures are also made to resemble minnows, small fish, or frogs.

The simplest type of spin bug one can make is a small popping bug much along the same lines as the popping plugs covered in the previous chapter. However, the spin bugs are much smaller, shorter, and have fewer hooks. And they will have hair or feathers added to imitate the legs or wings of a bug or insect.

The popping spin bug illustrated in Fig. 19 can be made from soft, light wood such as cedar or basswood. It should be about 11/2 in. long and 7/8 in. in diameter. The head slants downward at the regular 45-degree angle. You need two small screw-eyes and one treble hook to finish this bug. One screw eye goes at the head for the fishing line, while the other one holds the treble hook at the tail. The screw eyes and hooks should be smaller than those used for the regular fresh-water plugs discussed in Chapter 2; a No. 2 or No. 4 treble hook is a good size to use. The hooks should be sharp, fine-wire types of the best quality. You'll hook more fish with needle-sharp hooks than with dull, cheap ones.

Before the treble hook is put on the screw eye it should be wound with bucktail hair, as shown in Fig. 20. First cut your bucktail hair so that it is only slightly longer than the shank of the hook. Next, get some fly-tying thread and make a few turns with it around the hook shank near the eye. Now form three or four pinches of the bucktail hair and have them ready. Take one of the pinches of bucktail, lay it against the hook shank, and wind several turns of thread around it. Add another pinch of bucktail next to the

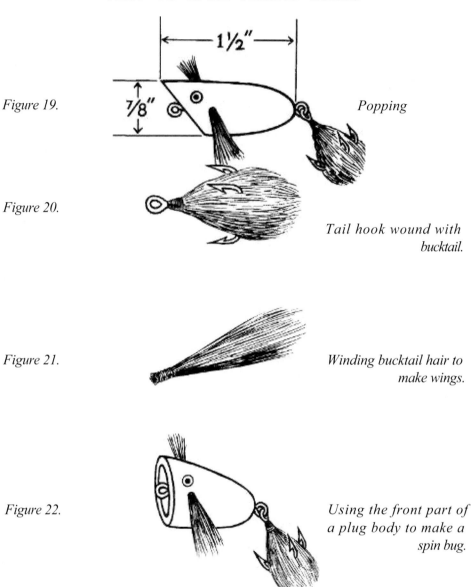

Figure 19.   Popping

Figure 20.

Tail hook wound with
bucktail.

Figure 21.   Winding bucktail hair to
make wings.

Figure 22.   Using the front part of
a plug body to make a
spin bug.

first one and wind some thread around it. Keep doing this until the hook
shank is completely covered by the bucktail. Finish off the wrapping with
more turns and bind it with a whip finish or a series of half hitches. Then
coat the thread wrapping with fly-tying cement or with one of the clear,
quick-drying cements which come in tubes.

To make the wings of the spin bug which project from the sides, use buck-tail or other hair. Take two pinches of the bucktail and wrap the butts tightly wih fly-tying thread, as shown in Fig. 21. Then dip or dab the windings with clear, waterproof cement. After they dry, drill two holes in the wood body of the bug, one on each side. When you do this, make sure that the holes are just big enough to take the butts of the bucktail wings snugly. In other words, it should be a tight fit. Then dip the butts of the wings in clear cement and insert them into the holes. You can also force a drop or two of the cement into the holes with a stick or brush. When the cement dries the bucktail wings will be held firmly in place.

Another type of popping spin bug can be made, using the plug body of the popping plug described in the previous chapter. Only here you cut off the tail section so that the bug is short, as shown in Fig. 22. This bug can also have a treble hook wound with bucktail hair and wings at the sides.

SIDE VIEW   TOP VIEW

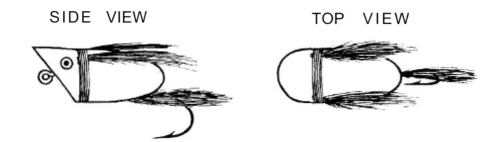

Popping spin bug with a single hook.   *Figure 23.*

BOTTOM VIEW

Hole and slot in a bug, to take a hook.   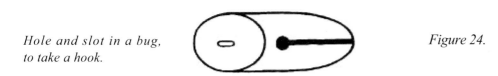   *Figure 24.*

SIDE VIEW

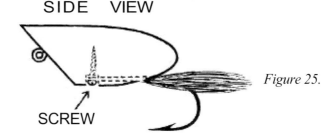

Single hook inserted in hole and slot.   *Figure 25.*

SCREW

A third kind of popping spin bug is shown in Fig. 23. For this one you use the same size wooden body as the popping bug shown in Fig. 19. However, instead of attaching a free-swinging treble hook you add a single hook to the underside of the body. A regular shank hook about size No. 2/0 can be used. To attach this hook, first drill a shallow hole underneath the body, about half inch from the tail end. This hole should be large enough to take the round eye of the hook. The next step is to slit a narrow groove in the wood, running from the hole to the end of the body. This will accommodate the hook shank. See Fig. 24. Now wind some bucktail on the hook shank, about a half inch from the eye of the hook, then force the hook eye and shank into the hole and slot. After this, get a small screw and screw it through the hook eye. This will hold the hook firmly in place. See Fig. 25. Then get some plastic wood and fill up the hole and slit to conform to the round body shape of the bug. To complete the bug, wrap on two bucktail or feather wings on the top or sides of the bug body. The tying thread can be wound completely around the body. Then dab some clear cement on the winding and paint over this winding when the cement dries, so that it doesn't show.

Such single hook spin bugs can easily be made weedless by adding a wire hook guard made from fine stainless steel or piano wire. Use a nail or thick wire to form the eye of the guard, as shown in Fig. 26. When making the single hook spin bug, this wire is slipped on the small screw first, then the hook. In other words, the same screw holds both the wire guard and the hook in place.

The next spin bug is a silent type which has a pointed nose instead of a cupped or slanted head. This type of bug resembles a minnow or some other

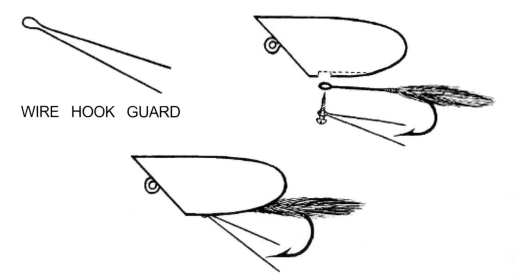

WIRE HOOK GUARD

Figure 26.   *Adding a wire hook guard to make a spin bug weedless.*

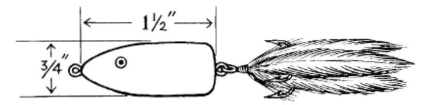

Silent type spin bug.   *Figure 27.*

kind of small fish more than it does a bug. It swims through the water creating a ripple like a minnow cleaving the surface of a stream or lake. The construction and dimensions of this lure are shown in Fig. 27. The wood body
should be about 1 1/2 in. long and 3/4 in. in diameter. The quick way to
make this bug is to fasten a screw eye in the nose and another one at the tail,
for free-swinging treble hook or a single hook. The treble will hook more
fish, but the single hook will snag less in the weeds. To give this bug a
minnow appearance the hook should be wrapped with four or six rooster
hackle feathers, long enough and wide enough to cover the treble (or single)
hook. When tying these feathers on the hook, wrap a few turns of the thread
under them to make them splay out. In other words, try to make the hackles
slant out away from the hook. This will give them a "breathing" action in
the water. If you want to, tie in another hackle feather near the hook eye,
then wind it around the hook to form a collar of hackle.

   To make a stronger bug of this type, run a wire through the wood body
from nose to tail and form eyes at each end to take the line and the hook.
And, instead of using hackle feathers, tie some long bucktail hairs around
the hook shank.

   A somewhat heavier and larger type of spin bug can be made, as shown
in Fig. 28. This is also a minnow type of lure since it is shaped more like a
small fish than an insect. However, if you want to do so, it can be dressed
up with wings or other hair or feathers on the body, to resemble a very large
bug. The way it stands with a streamlined body and only a few feathers on
the hook makes it an excellent casting lure when used with a spinning outfit. The body can be about 2V2 in. long and % in. in diameter at the thickest

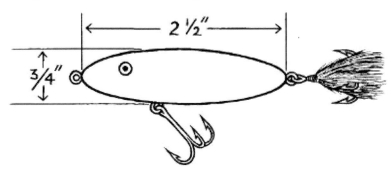

Minnow type spin bug.   *Figure 28.*

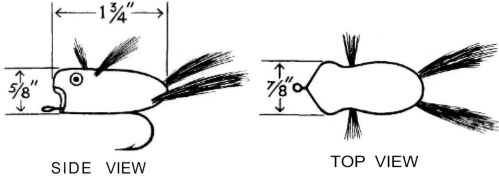

SIDE VIEW   TOP VIEW

Figure 29.   *Frog type spin bug.*

part in the center. It tapers to a rounded nose and tail on both ends. Small
screw eyes can be used at the nose, under the belly and at the tail to hold
the two treble hooks. The rear treble hook can be wound with short bucktail hair.

Spin bugs can also be made to imitate small frogs, which are a favorite
food of black bass, pickerel, and pike. You can easily make such a bug as
shown in Fig. 29. The wood body should be 1 3/4 in. long and about 7/8 in.
wide; in depth it can be about 5/8 in. thick. The head is cut out, as shown in
the side-view drawing in Fig. 29. To make this lure you need a regular-
length shank hook with a hump such as those used for tying cork bass bugs.
First, wrap the hook shank with fine fly tying thread, and then cut a slot in the
belly of the wood body to accommodate the hook. Make sure that you cut a
groove deep enough to take the hump of the hook. The next step is to put
some clear quick-drying cement both on the wrapped hook shank and inside
the slot of the wood body. You can use a thin knife blade to push this cement into the slot. Force the hook shank into the slot of the wood body and
fix it in its permanent position. When the cement dries, fill the slot with
plastic wood. To finish off this bug, drill holes near the head to add a couple
of short pinches of bucktail hair to simulate legs, and then drill two more
holes near the tail and insert two longer pinches of bucktail to simulate legs.

The spin bugs described above are made from wood and have enough
weight to cast with a light spinning or casting outfit. You can also make
them from cork, but you'll have to add some lead to provide enough weight
for casting. For this you will need some sheet lead and lead wire. If you
have trouble getting sheet lead you can always get some lead sinkers and
pound them flat with a hammer. Lead wire can be obtained from some of
the mail-order supply houses.

Before we go into the methods of loading a cork bug with lead we will
describe the basic construction of such a bug. You can obtain cork cylinders
or cork bass bug bodies, already shaped and sanded smooth, from the mail-

order houses and fly-tying suppliers. They come in various lengths and thicknesses, but for best results use the largest sizes.

To make a cork bug you'll need long shank double-hump hooks, as shown in Fig. 30. Sizes 1/0 and 2/0 are best for spin bugs. The hook shank is then wrapped with fine fly-tying thread along the section which will be buried in the cork body. This wrapping provides a better gripping surface than the smooth metal of the bare hook.

The next step is to cut a slot along the bottom of the cork lengthwise, to take the hook. This can be done with a single-edge razor blade, or you can use a small saw such as a hacksaw. This slot should be just deep enough to bury the hook shank in the body. See Fig. 31. Another method often used is to cut out a triangular wedge along the bottom, as shown in Fig. 31. Whichever method you use, coat the wrapped hook shank with clear, waterproof cement and, if you have a slot in your cork body, also force some cement into it. Some anglers prefer to use a waterproof marine glue such as the plastic resin type instead of the clear cement. Both are good, although the plastic resin glue is somewhat stronger and more permanent.

After the hook shank has been covered with cement and you have worked some of the cement into the cork body, force the hook into the slot. Then wrap the cork body fairly tightly with some cord to press the slot together while the cement dries.

If you cut a triangular wedge out of your cork body, coat your hook shank with cement or glue and push it in place, into the cork body. Then add more cement or glue to the area which has been cut out and also to the wedge itself. Put the triangular wedge back in place and tie some cord around the cork body to hold it in place while drying.

To add lead weight to a cork spin bug, use a cork body shaped like a bottle stopper. In other words, don't round off the tail part but leave it flat like a cork bottle stopper. Then cut a round piece from a sheet of lead to fit neatly at the tail end of the cork body. If you are using a single hook on your spin bug, cut a small slot in the lead so that the weight can be slipped over the hook. Then drill a hole in the center of the round lead weight to accommodate a small screw. Now coat both the tail end of the cork body and the lead weight with cement and screw the lead piece in place on the cork. See Fig. 32.

If you are making a spin bug with a treble hook instead of a single hook, you go through the same steps. Of course, you do not need a slot in the lead weight now—only a small hole in the center of the round lead. You slip this lead onto the wire used in the "through-the-body" construction of this type of spin bug, then form a wire eye at the tail to take the hook. You can also cement or glue the lead weight onto the cork body, but the wire eye will keep it in position.

When making a spin bug with a pointed or rounded tail, wait until the lure is finished with feathers or hair. Then get some of the lead wire and

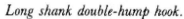

Figure 30.   *Long shank double-hump hook.*

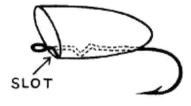

SLOT

SECTION CUT FROM BODY

Figure 31.   *Cork bug bodies prepared for the hook.*

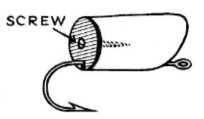

SCREW

LEAD WEIGHT WITH
HOLE AND SLOT

WEIGHT IN PLACE
ON CORK BODY

Figure 32.   *Adding a lead weight to a cork bug.*

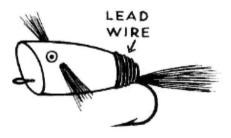

LEAD
WIRE

LEAD WIRE

Figure 33.   *Cork bugs weighted with lead wire.*

wind it around the hook shank next to the cork body, or wind the lead wire around the cork body itself. See Fig. 33. In any of these operations, always make sure you do not add too much lead weight. Otherwise, the cork body will sit too low in the water or will be cocked at the wrong angle.

To finish off the cork spin bugs, add hackle feathers at the tail and wings on the body, as described for the wood type spin bugs above.

In painting any of the wood or cork body spin bugs use enamels or lacquers. If you want to, dip the body three or four times in the color. Or, if you have an airbrush, spray the bugs. A quick way to paint them is to use the fast-drying "dope" used by model airplane builders. This comes in many colors and you can add one coat after another in a short time. Wood will require only two or three coats, but cork is more porous and rougher and may take more coats.

You can use any color combinations you want on bugs, but the most effective ones are usually black body and wings, brown body and wings, or yellow body and wings. A bug with white body and white tail or wings is easily seen and is as good as any. When making the silent minnow-type bug, use silver or gold paint on the sides of the body. The frog-type can have a white or yellow belly and green back with black spots.

You can also give spin bugs a fuzzy or hair finish on the body. This is done by first painting the bug the color you want, then giving it a coat of clear cement or celluloid enamel. Then, while it is still wet, sprinkle with bits of hair, wool or floss. These materials, of course, have to be prepared in advance by cutting or chopping up the hair, wool, or fur finely.

Still another finish on spin bugs can be obtained by using flitters. These are small metallic chips of gold or silver which can be scattered on the wet coat of cement or clear celluloid enamel of the bug body. They are given a coat of clear lacquer afterwards, to prevent the metallic chips from tarnishing.

Although many bugs made professionally have glass eyes, these are not really necessary. It is much quicker and less expensive to paint on the eyes or dab them on, as described and shown in Chapter 2. You can also obtain decal eyes from some of the fly-tying and mail-order houses and attach these quickly.

Salt-Water Plugs

There are many reasons why you should make your own salt-water fishing plugs. First, of course, is to save some money since the larger plugs are quite expensive if purchased. Anglers lose more salt-water plugs than fresh-water plugs. It is possible to fish with one plug in fresh-water for many years. But you're lucky if you don't lose some salt-water plugs in a few days of fishing. The fishing line may break on a cast, or the plug gets tangled in rocks, piles, or weeds. Also, the big salt-water fish are always breaking lines and taking the plugs with them. Finally, the wear and tear on salt-water plugs quickly ruins the paint and the wood body and rusts the hooks. A salt-water fisherman continually has to replace lost or ruined plugs.

Furthermore, fishing with salt-water plugs is comparatively new. Fishing with such plugs didn't really become popular until after World War II, so there is still plenty of room for experimentation. Many salt-water anglers, especially surf anglers, are always trying to create new plugs or improve the old ones. They add stronger hooks, rearrange hooks, make plugs of different shapes, sizes, and weights, and try out different color schemes.

Salt-water plugs can also be made from cedar, and this is the best wood to use for the smaller type plugs. This light wood has the buoyancy to support metal parts such as lips, screw eyes, screws, and hooks without sinking. The use of cedar is especially important when making surface plugs. But cedar may be too light for the larger-sized salt-water plugs, unless loaded with lead. Hence, many surf anglers who use big plugs make them from heavier woods such as birch, fir, maple, and walnut. Even such hard woods as ash, oak, and hickory have been used when a heavy salt-water plug is required. However, these woods are tough to cut, drill, or shape with hand tools, and they do not support too many hardware parts without sinking. In fact, when making any salt-water surface plugs it is necessary to check carefully to make certain that the wood body will support the metal plates, screw eyes, hooks, and other hardware without sinking. All surface plugs should float for best results. I find it's a good idea to assemble all the metal parts which will go on a certain plug and strap them on the wood body with a rubber band. Then place the wooden plug body in a pail or bathtub filled with water. If it doesn't sink or submerge too much, you are safe in using all that metal on the plug. Otherwise, you have to make a larger wooden body or use lighter screws, screw-eyes, metal plates, or hooks.

In salt-water fishing the deadliest type of plug is usually a surface model. The easiest plug of this type to make is the simple popper shown in Fig. 34. This plug can be about 6 1/2 in. long and have a diameter of 1 1/8, in. The head can be straight cut at a 45-degree angle. The plug is equipped with three 5/0 extra-strong treble hooks. The quickest way to attach these hooks to the body is by means of screw eyes, which should be fairly large and of heavy wire with long, deep threads. The best screw eyes are made of brass since they don't rust in salt water. However, you can use galvanized iron screws if they are heavy and strong. If this popper is made from a heavy wood it will cast far without additional weight. But if you use light wood or want as heavy a plug as possible, add some lead to the tail end of the plug as shown in Fig. 35. You drill a hole and plug it up with a round chunk of lead. If you make a tight fit you can tap in the lead after putting some cement in the hole.

Heavy screw eyes will usually prove satisfactory as hook holders and for attaching the line to the plugs described here. For stronger plugs, however, attach the hooks by using hook hangers similar to the one used for fresh-water plugs. For salt-water plugs, such a hook hanger must be heavier than that used for fresh-water plugs. You can make such hook hangers by using a brass piece I 1/2 in. long by 1/4 in. wide and 1/32 in. thick. File the brass in a bench vise as shown in Fig. 36. Then bend it with round-nosed and flat-nosed pliers so that the finished hook hanger will look like the one shown in the illustration.

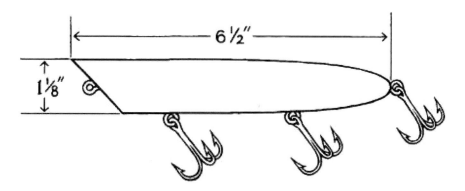

Simple type of salt-water popper plug. *Figure 34.*

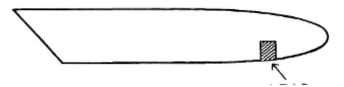

Position of lead weight in plug body. *Figure 35.*

FILE LIKE THIS   BEND LIKE THIS

Making a hook hanger from brass stock.

To make the salt-water plugs still stronger, use the "through-wire" construction method shown in Fig. 37. Here you drill a hole through the center of the plug body from the nose to the tail. Then drill larger-diameter holes in the belly of the plug which meet the smaller hole through the middle of the body. Next, make some hook hangers from brass or stainless steel wire. See the illustration, of such a hook hanger in Fig. 38. Then get about a 10-in. length of brass wire or stainless steel wire, form an eye on one end, and insert the other end of the wire in the nose of the plug. Attach a treble hook

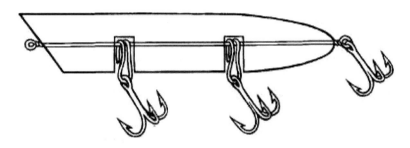

Figure 37.   *Through-wire construction and wire hook hangers.*

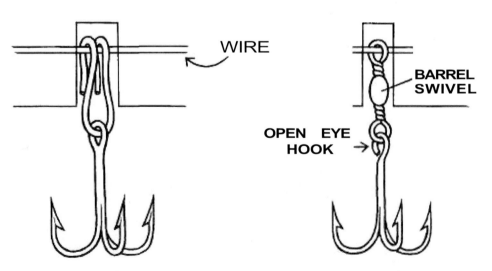

Figure 38.   *Two types of hook hangers used with through-wire construction plugs.*

to one of the hook hangers and insert this into the hole at the belly of the plug. At the same time, push the wire rod through the plug to catch this hook hanger through the double loop. You can easily test to see that the hanger is caught on the wire by pulling on the treble hook. After the first treble is caught, insert the second hanger and hook and catch that with the wire and then push the wire out through the rear of the plug. To finish it, form an eye at the tail, but before closing the eye slide on another treble hook.

Instead of making a wire hook hanger, you can use barrel swivels for hook hangers, as shown in Fig. 38. They have two eyes; the eye inside the body of the plug is caught by the wire and the eye outside the plug holds the hook. To attach the hooks you must either obtain treble hooks which can be opened at the eye or cut the eye with strong cutting pliers or hacksaw. You can also attach the hook to the barrel swivel eye by first forcing on a split ring, then attaching the hook to this ring. If you use brass split rings you can solder them so that they can't open.

Another strong way to attach a treble hook to a wooden plug is to drill holes in the belly and tail of the plug to take hook hangers. Then drill smaller-diameter holes from one side of the plug body to the other. Care must be taken here to meet the larger hole. Then insert the hook hanger, or barrel swivel with treble hook, into the big hole. Finally, drive a brass or copper pin through the small hole to catch the hook hanger or barrel swivel eye.

Another large popper which you can make is shown in Fig. 39. This has a tapered body about 7 in. long and a diameter of 1V4 in. at the head. The head is cupped or gouged out to create a commotion and splash in the water when the plug is jerked. This plug can have three 5/0 or 6/0 treble hooks, two at the belly and one at the tail. They can be attached by any of the methods described above. The plug can be loaded at the belly or tail with lead, if you want.

A somewhat smaller popper is the bomber type shown in Fig. 40. This one is narrow at the head and thicker in diameter at the tail. Because of this

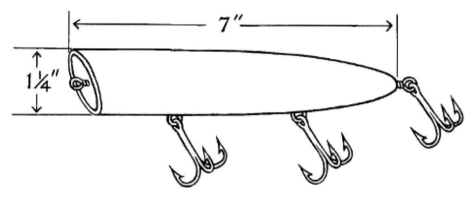

Popper with cupped head.   *Figure 39.*

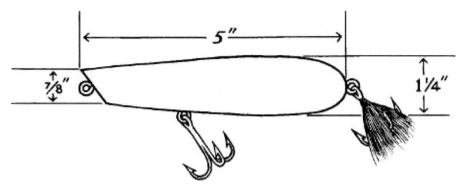

Figure 40.   *Bomb type popper.*

shape, it casts like a bullet even into a stiff wind. The plug shown here is heavy enough to use with a conventional surf rod or with a surf spinning outfit. It measures about 5 in. long and has a diameter of 1 1/4 in. at the tail and 7/8 in. at the head. The head is cut at a slant of 45 degrees. Two 5/0 treble hooks are attached, one at the belly near the head and the other at the tail.

The large surface plugs described above are mostly used for surf fishing or casting, or trolling for big fish with fairly heavy tackle. If you want to make up smaller salt-water surface plugs to use with light spinning or casting tackle just make a smaller version of any of the models above. For example, if you want a small surface popper of the type shown in Fig. 41, make it the same way as the large one (Fig. 39), but smaller and lighter. It could have a body 4 in. long with a diameter of 7/8 in. Instead of using three treble hooks, you need only two and these can be smaller. Size 1/0 or 2/0 hooks are best, but make sure they are of heavy wire and strong.

Another effective surface popper can be made by using the same size plug body as the fresh-water wobbler plug shown in Fig. 1, page 13. However, instead of using it as shown, turn the body around and use it as in Fig. 42. Now, instead of diving or wobbling, it becomes a small surface popper which throws a big splash when jerked. It also can use two treble hooks in sizes 1/0 or 2/0.

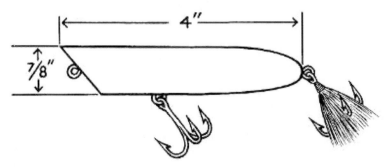

Figure 41.   *Small salt-water popper.*

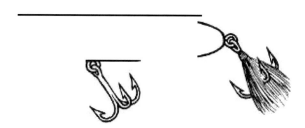

Popper made from wobbler type body.   *Figure 42.*

You can use the surface popper plugs above as they are, or you can tie some white or yellow bucktail hair around the treble hook at the tail. Do not put on too much hair, especially on the smaller and lighter plugs, or you won't get as much distance on the cast.

Other surface salt-water plugs include the swimming type shown in Fig. 43. This plug can have a body about 6 1/2 in. long and a diameter of *IV** in. at the head. It tapers at the tail to about 5/8 in. This plug has a metal lip of the type and size shown in Fig. 44, which can be cut from sheet brass or stainless steel. If you use stainless steel, you can use a lighter gauge than if you use brass because it has more spring. The metal lip is bent and a hole is drilled as shown. For this plug the through-wire construction is most prac-

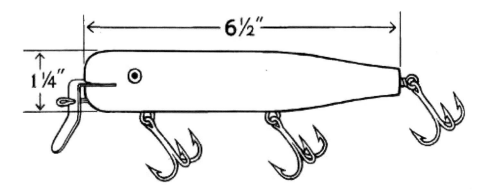

Swimming type surface plug.   *Figure 43.*

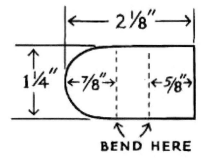

BEND HERE

BEND LIKE THIS

Metal lip for swimming type surface plug.   *Figure 44.*

tical to hold the metal lip and the three 5/0 treble hooks in place. The wire used for this construction is bent into a loop to form the eye in front of the lip and plug, as shown in the illustration. To assemble this plug, first cut a slit at the head of the plug body to accept the metal lip, then drill a hole for the wire to run through the body. This hole is slightly off center at the head of the plug and through the center at the tail.

Still another surface plug is the flaptail type with a revolving tail. This is shown in Fig. 45. It can have a body 6 1/2 in. long and a diameter of 1 1/8 in. The tail tapers to about 5/s in., and the head is cut slightly at a slant on top. This plug has a metal tail of the type and size shown in Fig. 46, cut out of

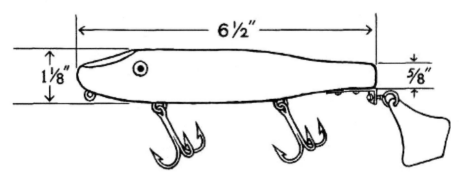

Figure 45.   *Flaptail surface plug.*

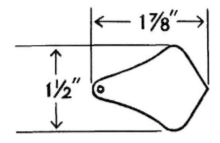

Figure 46.   *Metal flaptail.*

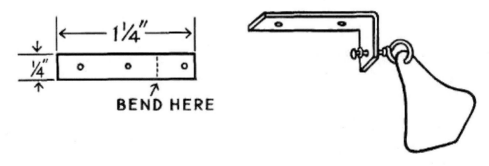

Figure 47.   *Metal bracket for holding flaptail.*

sheet brass. To attach this tail to the plug, use a small metal bracket about 1 1/4 in. long and V4 in. wide. This can also be cut from sheet brass. After it is cut out, it is bent about 3/8 of an inch from the end, after a hole has been drilled. A long brass wire nail is inserted in this hole. Before you do this, however, add a small brass nut or washer next to the head of the long nail, to serve as a bearing. Then slip the metal tail on the nail and form an eye with pliers to hold the tail. Next, drill two holes in the bracket and fasten it with two screws at the tail of the wooden plug body. The details showing how this part is made are in Fig. 47. To finish off this plug, add two treble hooks at the belly and a screw eye at the nose to which you tie the fishing line.

Another very effective salt-water surface plug is the "torpedo" type shown in Fig. 48. This plug can be about 4 1/2 in. long and 7/8 in. in diameter at its thickest part. It tapers at both ends and has two treble hooks in sizes 1 /0 or 2/0, one attached at the tail and the other at the belly. A screw eye is attached to the nose for the fishing line.

Salt-water anglers have also found the "darter" type plugs very effective for many fish. You can make a small one to use with light spinning or casting tackle in the same size as the fresh-water darter shown in Fig. 11, page 17. But for the salt-water model, you should use longer and stronger screw eyes with heavy wire hooks.

To make a larger darter plug for surf fishing or to use with heavy salt-water tackle follow the dimensions shown in Fig. 49. The body can be 6V2

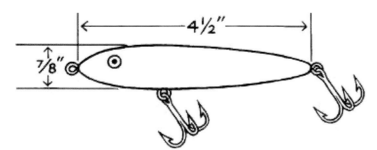

Torpedo plug.   Figure 48.

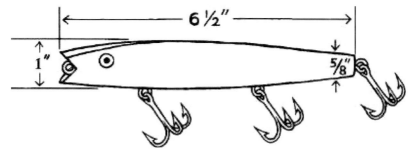

Darter plug.   Figure 49.

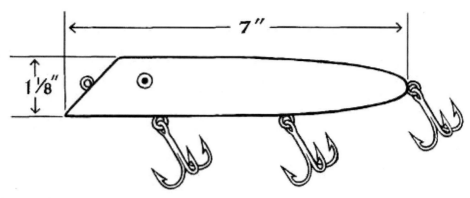

Figure 50.   *Large wobbler plug.*

in. long and an inch in diameter. The tail tapers to about 5/8 in. The top of the plug slopes downward toward the nose, where there is a triangular cut. A screw eye is screwed in this cut to hold the fishing line. Three treble hooks in size 5/0 are attached, two at the belly and one at the tail.

A large "wobbler" plug suitable for surf fishing is shown in Fig. 50. It can have a body 7 in. long with a diameter of 1 1/8 in. at the head and tapering to about 5/8 in. at the tail. The head is cut at a slant of 45 degrees. This plug also carries three 5/0 treble hooks, two at the belly and one at the tail. A large screw eye at the head holds the fishing line.

Finally, we have the "underwater" plug shown in Fig. 51. This has a body 7 in. long and a diameter of 1 3/8 in. at its thickest part. It tapers sharply toward the head and more gradually toward the tail. This plug has a metal lip of the size and shape shown in Fig. 52. If you use the through-wire construction method all you have to do is bend the lip as shown and drill a hole for the wire loop which will form the eye.

Another way to attach this lip is shown in Fig. 53. You make and bend the metal lip the same way, but drill three holes as shown. Then get a long brass wire nail, insert it into the single hole in the center of the lip, and bend

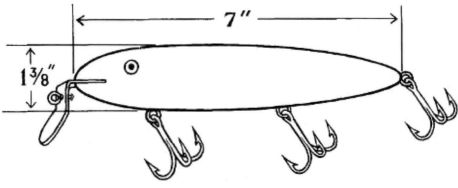

Figure 51.   *Underwater plug.*

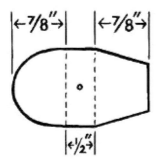

Metal lip for underwater plug.

BEND LIKE THIS

Figure 52.

BRASS PIN

Forming an eye for the metal lip.

Figure 53.

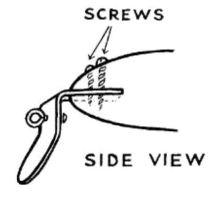

SCREWS

SIDE VIEW

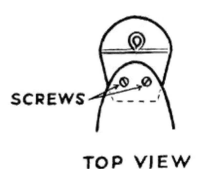

SCREWS

TOP VIEW

Using screws to attach lip to plug.

Figure 54.

with round-nosed pliers to form an eye for the fishing line. To attach this lip to the plug body, cut a slit to take the metal lip and drill two holes through the nose of the plug to meet the holes in the metal lip. Use two round-head brass screws to fasten the metal lip in place. See Fig. 54. This plug also takes three 5/0 treble hooks, two at the belly and one at the tail.

Salt-water plugs can be painted or sprayed in the same way as the fresh-water plugs, using the methods described in previous chapters. Choose any color combinations you like, but for surf fishing you'll find the "blue mullet" finish one of the best. To get this finish, the plug is first painted white, then a blue back is added blending into the white along the sides. Another popular salt-water color combination is blue and silver, the blue on the back and the silver along the sides. A silver scale finish can also be sprayed. Or it can be a solid silver finish.

When making your salt-water plugs it is very important to use the best quality and strongest salt-water treble hooks you can obtain. Strong hooks are the only ones which will stand up any length of time in salt water. Light wire hooks are easily straightened out by big fish, and rust weakens them in a short time.

The basic salt-water plugs described above will take care of most fishing needs. But don't let that stop you from experimenting with different shapes, sizes, or weights. Although it is easier to duplicate existing models of plugs, more satisfaction is obtained if you design your own. And there is always the chance that it will turn out to be a better fish-getter than existing plugs on the market.

Spoons

The spoon is one of the best lures the angler can use in fresh- or salt-water fishing. It is compact and heavy enough to cast well especially in the smaller sizes. It can be used when casting or trolling, and attracts all kinds of fish because of its brilliant "flash" and lively, swaying action.

The spoon is also one of the oldest fishing lures used by man, having its origins in the dim past. The lure we know as the spoon was used a long time ago in the Scandinavian countries. In this country the spoon was developed and perfected in the early 1800's. The story goes that a fisherman named Julio T. Buel dropped a teaspoon into the water. As he watched it twist and turn it gave him an idea. He started experimenting and soldered a hook to the end of another teaspoon and attached his line to the handle, which was partly cut off. It caught fish and then he went into the business of making spoons for fishermen.

You can make a spoon lure of sorts by merely taking a teaspoon or table-spoon and cut off the handle. Holes can be drilled at each end for holding the hook and line. Such a homemade spoon lure will catch fish, but is too deeply dished and the action is not the best. A much better spoon can be made by following the design shown in Fig. 55. This is one of the basic designs patterned after the famous "Dardevle" copied by many fishing tackle manufacturers.

To make a fresh-water spoon from scratch you have obtain brass or copper sheet metal in various thicknesses. The smaller-size spoons which run only from IV2 to 2½ in. in length use thinner-gauge metal than the larger spoons which measure from 3 to 5 in. in length.

This metal must be cut out and filed out to the size desired, then bent and hammered into the proper concave shape. This is a lot of work if done with hand tools, and takes time even with the aid of power tools. Then the holes to take the hooks and line have to be drilled. If the hook is soldered to the spoon that's another operation. Next, you have the spoons plated in nickel, chrome, gold, or silver. Or, if you want to use the brass or copper of the original metal, you must polish or buff it.

Frankly, when one figures the time, energy, and money spent in making fresh-water spoons from the raw material it really doesn't pay—not unless one is willing to go to the expense of having a die made to stamp out the spoons on a punch press. With such a die one can stamp out enough spoons to last a lifetime. Such a die runs into quite a bit of money and unless you need hundreds or thousands of spoons it isn't worth it.

Figure 55.

SPLIT RING
SIDE VIEW

Common type of fresh-water spoon.

Fortunately, you don't have to go to the trouble of shaping your own fresh-water spoons or spend money for expensive dies. Some of the mail-order houses carry spoons in various sizes, shapes, and weights. They are all complete with shiny gold, silver, brass, copper, chrome, or painted finishes and can be bought cheaply, especially in larger quantities. You can buy a dozen of the spoons and the other parts, such as split rings and hooks, and then assemble the spoons.

Split rings come in various sizes; the smaller ones are used for small spoons while the larger ones are needed for the bigger spoons. They are usually made from spring steel or solid brass. The steel split rings are plated and are suitable for fresh-water spoons, but for salt-water the solid brass rings are much better.

Fig. 56 shows how to use a knife blade to spread a split ring apart so that it can be forced into the hole on the spoon. Once you have the split ring started, just keep turning it until it snaps on completely. You can put two split rings on most spoons, one in front for the fishing line and the other in the back, to which a treble hook is attached. The treble hook can be plain or it can be wound with bucktail hair.

Although spoons with metal finishes are the most popular you can paint them in various colors—such as all white, all yellow, or red and white stripes —if you want to do so. Usually only the convex side is painted, the concave side retaining the metal silver or nickel finish. You can also paint or spray the convex side with a natural fish-scale finish. For painting by hand with a brush, enamels are best. For spraying, use the quicker drying lacquers. Clear lacquer or varnish can also be sprayed on a metal finish to keep it from tarnishing.

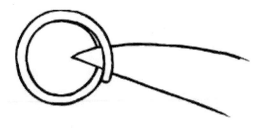

Figure 56.   *Using knife blade to open split ring.*

Although it doesn't pay to cut or stamp out your own fresh-water spoons, it's a different matter when we come to the larger salt-water spoons. These are more expensive and it often pays to make your own. Also, you cannot buy the larger metal spoon bodies already stamped out and plated, as you can the smaller fresh-water ones. So you either buy the finished spoon or make your own.

For pounding and shaping salt-water spoons you need a wooden anvil, which is nothing but a rectangular block of wood. Any block of hard wood such as oak or Douglas fir, about 12 in. long and 5 or 6 in. thick, is suitable. Toward one end of the block, drill a big hole and insert a peg of hard wood. You can also dig out some shallow holes and grooves along the working faces of the wood block. See Fig. 57. When shaping a spoon lay the sheet metal on the peg or over the shallow holes and pound it with a wooden mallet. See Fig. 58.

As an aid in shaping the metal, make some punches out of hard wood. The sheet metal is placed over the hole or groove on the wood block and the punch is held at the spot where you want the metal to be formed. Then strike the wood punch with the mallet to shape the spoon.

The metal for making spoons can be sheet brass, copper, or stainless steel. Stainless steel is being used more and more, and is especially suitable for salt-water spoons because it doesn't corrode or tarnish. But stainless steel, especially in the heavier gauges, is very hard and springy and tough to work with hand tools. If you have a workshop with power tools you can work with stainless steel. But if you do not have power tools and must use hand tools, you'll find it easier to work with brass, copper, or other soft metals.

Spring brass is a good metal and if you obtain sheets of this material in 1/32 in. thickness you'll be able to make varied sizes of spoons for salt-water fishing. Of course, slightly lighter gauges can be used for the smaller spoons and heavier gauges are more suitable for the larger spoons. The metal used should have enough spring so that it doesn't bend out of shape too readily when a big fish is hooked.

The first step in making a spoon is to draw and cut out a pattern of the shape and size you want from a piece of cardboard or heavy paper. This way, all your spoons will be uniform in size and you don't have to make a new drawing to follow each time. Then trace the pattern outline on the sheet metal. The lighter gauges of brass or copper can be cut with ordinary hand snips, and the heavier gauges can be cut with aviation snips. The duck bill snips are best for cutting the curves. You can also use a hacksaw or other metal saw to remove excess metal. When cutting out the spoons the best procedure is to cut just outside the tracing, leaving some metal. In other words, cut the spoon slightly larger in size than the finished one will be. Then file the spoon down to the finished size.

The shape and size of the spoon will depend, of course, on the type of fishing you do, the weight desired, and the size of the fish to be caught. The

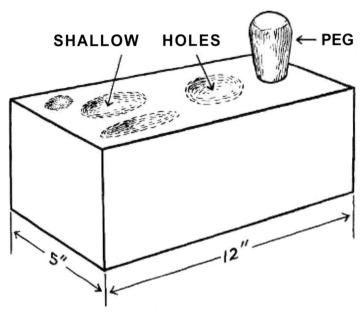

Figure 57.   *Wood block for shaping spoons.*

Figure 58.   *Using the wood block to shape a spoon.*

blade can be long and narrow, bigger at the head or at the tail. It can be short and broad and rounded at both ends, or you can shape it like a fish, with two fins and a tail. You can take almost any spoon and make a duplicate of it, or you can design your own. Fig. 59 shows some of the different shapes which can be used when making spoons.

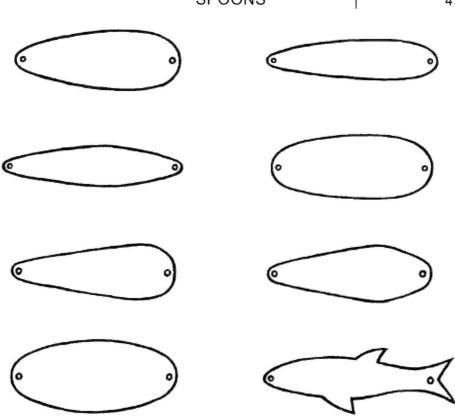

Shapes of spoons.   *Figure 59.*

Two basic types of spoons are usually made for salt-water fishing. One is based on the principle of the reverse S curve. See Fig. 60, left. Here the spoon is curved in one direction at the head and in the opposite direction at the tail. Both the head and tail are also hollowed or dished. The type of action you want will depend on how much of a curve you give the spoon. A spoon with a slight curve will have a somewhat faster wobble or wriggle than one which has extreme curves. The spoon with sharp curves and deep hollows will have more throw or sway when reeled or trolled. Naturally, experimentation will show just how much to curve or dish a spoon. Before you shape too many spoons, try one out in the water to see if it has the desired action.

The other basic type of spoon is the more conventional shape shown in Fig. 60, right. Here the spoon is curved and dished both from the head to the tail and from side to side. This type usually is wider at the head and tapers toward the tail.

The size of the spoon will depend on the type of fishing you do and the fish you seek. Small spoons measuring only 3 or 4 in. long are best for casting and trolling for small salt-water fish. Medium-sized spoons from 4 to 8 in. can be cast with heavier outfits or trolled for bigger fish. Some of the

Figure 60.   *Two basic curves of spoons.*

larger spoons, such as the so-called "bunker" spoons, run up to 12 in. in length and are used for big fish such as striped bass.

The hook used on a salt-water spoon should be strong enough and heavy enough to hold big fish. A single hook is better than a treble hook.

There are various ways to attach the hook to a spoon. The easiest and quickest way is the method usually used on fresh-water spoons, explained earlier. You drill one hole in the head and another in the tail, and insert split rings. Then you slip a big single hook on the split ring at the tail. Solid brass split rings should be used for salt-water spoons, and as an added measure of security the rings should be soldered after they are on the spoon.

Another strong way to attach a hook is to cut a slot in the tail end of the spoon and insert the hook shank through it. You also drill a hole in the body of the spoon where the eye of the hook falls, insert a small bolt through the hole and the hook eye, and fasten it in place with a nut. This is shown in Fig. 61. The advantage of this method is that you can quickly remove an old rusted hook and attach a new one, if needed. For best results, use brass hardware to hold the hook.

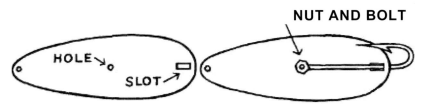

Figure 61.   *Attaching hook to spoon.*

If you use brass or copper sheet metal to make your spoons you can use them as they are by polishing them. A metal polish which can be bought in any hardware store can be used for this. However, the most effective finish for salt-water is a nickel-plated or chrome-plated spoon. For plating, you have to take the spoons to a shop which does metal plating, and do this before you assemble the spoons. Some anglers also paint their spoons silver, white, or yellow. Lacquers or enamel can be used for this. Of course, if you made your spoons from stainless steel all you have to do is polish them to a high gloss.

Naturally, home-made spoons will not look exactly like commercial ones. There will be slight imperfections in construction or the finish. But don't let that worry you. The fish don't know the difference and take them just as readily as the ones bought in a fishing tackle store.

Spinners

Somewhat similar to spoons are the spinners which revolve on a wire shaft or a swivel. They are also very effective lures for many fresh- and salt-water fish and an angler should always carry a good assortment of these lures. They are easy to make and very inexpensive when made at home.

Here again, it doesn't pay to make the spinner blades themselves. The time and effort spent in cutting them out isn't worth it because you can buy all the spinner blades you want from many of the mail-order supply houses. They have them in stock in various shapes, sizes, and finishes and also carry the other parts needed such as wire, swivels, beads, clevises, body forms and weights, and split rings. You can buy the spinner blades by the dozen, gross, or thousand lots. Some of the blades cost about one cent apiece in the larger quantities. These are already stamped, shaped, and plated. You couldn't possibly make them for much less by cutting out the blades from sheet metal and then plating them. By buying the finished blades and the other parts all you have to do is assemble the spinners.

Spinner blades come in various shapes such as the Indiana, Colorado, Willow Leaf, June Bug, Kidney, and Propeller types. See Fig. 62. They usually run in size from No. 00 to No. 7 and up. The lower the number, the smaller the blade. Numbers 00, 0, and 1 are small sizes suitable for trout and panfish, while the larger sizes are best for bass, pike, lake trout, and salt-water fish. You can get the spinner blades in various finishes such as gold, nickel, brass, and copper. Some are also made with hammered finishes. Still other blades are made from pearl or mussel shell.

To make completed spinners you also need spring steel or stainless steel wire for shafts. The spring steel wire is usually coated with tin and is quite suitable for fresh-water spinners. The stainless steel wire is better for salt-water spinners. This wire is supplied in various diameters from .018 to .035, the thin gauges being used for small spinners and the heavier gauges for the larger fresh-water spinners and all salt-water types.

You also need beads, which are used on the wire shafts to act as bearings. These beads are made from different materials and come in various sizes. The light beads, made from pearl, glass, plastic, or hollow metal, are used for most spinners where no extra weight is required. The solid brass beads are used for spinners which will be cast. Instead of solid metal beads you can use body forms made from solid metal to provide the weight. See Fig. 63. They can be ordered from fishing lure parts suppliers, or you can make

49

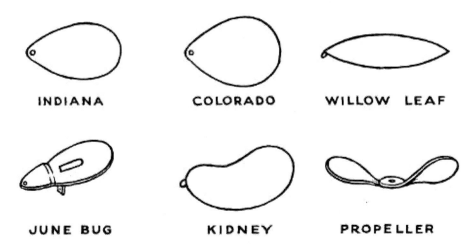

INDIANA   COLORADO   WILLOW LEAF

JUNE BUG   KIDNEY   PROPELLER

Figure 62.   *Shapes of spinner blades.*

your own by obtaining solid brass rods, then cutting them into short lengths
and drilling a hole through the center.

Spinners also require clevises, which hold the blade so that it can revolve
freely around the wire shaft. There are two types, as shown in Fig. 64. They
usually come in two or three different sizes for small and large spinners.

Split rings are also needed in various sizes when making spinners. Barrel
swivels such as those shown in Fig. 65 are also required in different sizes.
Some of these split rings and swivels can be bought in fishing tackle stores,

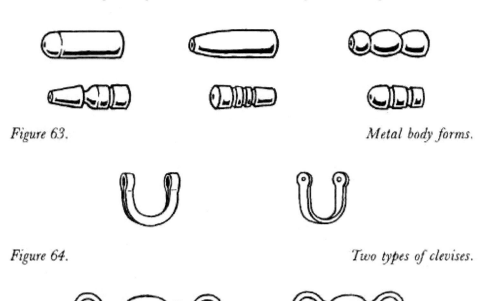

Figure 63.   *Metal body forms.*

Figure 64.   *Two types of clevises.*

Figure 65.   *Two types of barrel swivels.*

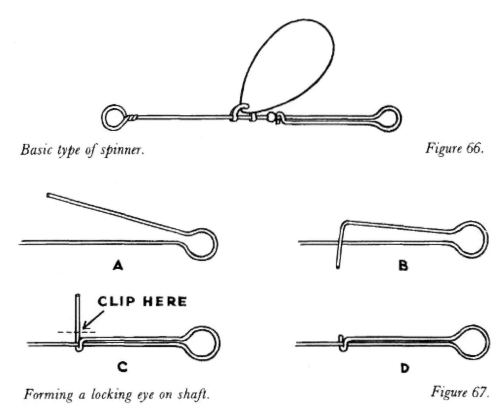

Basic type of spinner. *Figure 66.*

CLIP HERE

A   B
C   D

Forming a locking eye on shaft. *Figure 67.*

but you can save money if you buy them in larger quantities such as gross lots from a mail-order house.

The basic spinner, which can be used for trolling for many fish, is the Indiana blade on a short wire shaft shown in Fig. 66. To make this spinner, cut off a length of wire for the shaft and form a locking type eye on one end. For this you'll need diagonal cutting pliers and the round-nosed pliers (the small jeweler's round-nosed pliers are best for this work). The first step in making the locking eye is to form it with the round-nosed pliers about an inch from the end of the wire shaft. Then form the catch on the end of the wire. See Fig. 67 for the steps in doing this. Chapter 12 on leaders and connections will also give you tips on forming eyes and snaps for spinners.

After you have finished the locking eye, slide about two metal or glass beads on the shaft, then add the spinner blade on a clevis and slide it up the wire shaft. To finish the spinner, form an eye on the end of the shaft to which the leader or line will be attached. The spinner is ready for use after you add a plain or feathered treble hook to the locking eye at the tail.

Another way to attach the hook to the spinner is to use a sliding coil spring or sleeve which slides on the shaft up to the eye and holds the wire together. See Fig. 68. These coil springs and brass or copper sleeves can be bought in various diameters from the mail-order houses. Still another way to attach a hook to a spinner is to form a permanent closed eye on the end

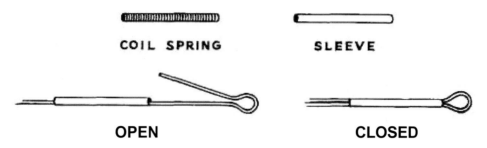

Figure 68.   *Using a coil spring or sleeve to close the eye on a shaft.*

of the wire, then slip on a split ring with a hook, as shown in Fig. 69. These methods of attaching a hook to a spinner are used if you plan to change the hook often. If, however, you want to make a stronger, permanent attachment you merely form an eye on the end of the wire shaft, slip on the treble hook, and then close the eye for good.

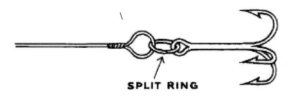

PERMANENT EYE

Figure 69.   *Permanent eye on a spinner shaft.*

The basic spinner above makes use of a single blade. If you want to add another blade to the shaft, use a slightly longer wire and after slipping on the first blade add a small metal bead which you then solder to the shaft above the first blade. Then slip on a loose bead or two and your second blade before forming the eye at the front of the wire shaft. This is shown in Fig. 70.

Another popular and effective spinner is the "June Bug" type shown in Fig. 71. The June Bug blade has an extension cut from the blade itself, and this keeps the blade revolving at a fixed distance from the shaft. This spinner works very freely and smoothly even at slow speeds. When making this type of spinner use the large red ruby cut glass beads as bearings on the shaft, and add a barrel swivel to which the line is tied. At the other end, attach a long-shank single hook such as the Carlisle pattern. Anglers usually use this spinner with the hook baited with a minnow, strip offish, pork rind, or a gob of worms. You can also make this spinner with two blades by using a longer wire shaft and adding a smaller blade up front, as shown in Fig. 72.

The propeller type of spinner shown in Fig. 73 is also good to use for trolling at slow speeds. You can buy the propeller blades in the largest sizes from the fishing lure parts suppliers. The two propeller blades used to make this spinner are spaced so that they revolve freely without interfering with each other. You have to solder a metal bead to the wire shaft to keep the

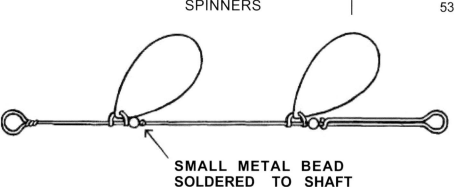

SMALL METAL BEAD SOLDERED TO SHAFT

Spinner with double blade.　　　　　　　　　　*Figure 70.*

Single-blade June bug spinner.　　　　　　　　*Figure 71.*

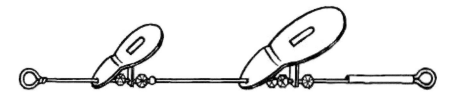

Double-blade June bug spinner.　　　　　　　　*Figure 72.*

first propeller blade away from the rear one. This type of spinner is usually used with a feathered treble hook attached behind it.

Another popular spinner is the type known as the "Cherry Bobber" or "Cherry Drifter" shown in Fig. 74. This spinner makes use of a wooden, pear-shaped body which gives it buoyancy and prevents it from sinking too fast. You can make these bodies from any light wood, but balsa is preferred because it is easy to work. You can also order these wood bodies, all ready shaped from a mail-order house. The wood body is then painted a bright red—a daylight fluorescent lacquer is best for this. Likewise, fluorescent plastic beads are slipped on the wire shaft to act as bearings. A small treble hook is attached to the tail end of the spinner.

Still another old-time favorite among spinners is the "Colorado" shown in Fig. 75. Here, instead of using a wire shaft, you use two barrel swivels and two split rings. The blade, which is the round type Colorado, is attached to the split ring as shown. The split ring at the tail holds either two single hooks or one treble hook.

Most of the spinners above are used for trolling, but they can also be cast

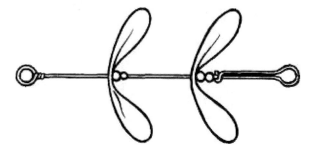

Figure 73.   *Propeller type spinner.*

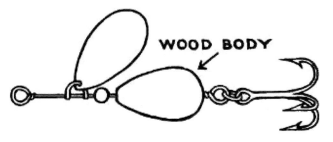

Figure 74.   *Cherry bobber spinner.*

Figure 75.   *Colorado type spinner.*

if you add a small clincher sinker or other weight to the leader. You can also get some sheet lead and cut out a small rudder which is then folded over the wire shaft of the spinner in front of the blade. See Fig. 76. To keep it from sliding down the shaft, make more turns than usual when forming the eye of the spinner. Then crimp the lead rudder on these turns with pliers. In addition to serving as a casting weight, the lead rudder also acts as a keel and prevents the spinner from twisting the line. You can paint this lead weight in any color you want and even add an eye on each side.

You can also make special casting or trolling weights which are detachable and can be added to the spinner at the front. See Chapter 11 on making sinkers for details on how such weights can be made.

For easy casting, however, you can't beat the "French" type of spinner shown in Fig. 77. These usually have short wire shafts on which one or more heavy brass body weights are added. These body weights come in various shapes, sizes, and designs shown in Fig. 63. French-type spinners also use a special heavier blade than the regular kinds. Both the body weights and blades can be ordered from many of the supply houses. These casting type spinners usually have a small treble hook attached.

Other casting type spinners use heavy brass beads for body weight, as shown in Fig. 78. These beads come in different sizes and are usually arranged as shown in the illustration. You can also use lead body weights which come in bullet, torpedo, or double taper shapes. See Fig. 79. They have a center hole and come in different weights and sizes. You can order such lead weights either unpainted or painted.

Another way to make spinners is to use nylon leader material instead of wire to serve as a shaft. You can buy the nylon material in coils of various diameters and strengths. Cut off a length, tie a loop for an eye up front, slip

Lead keel weight and its position in front of the spinner blade.   *Figure 76.*

French type spinner.   *Figure 77.*

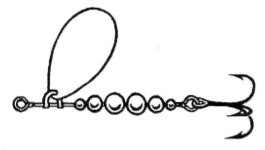

Spinner with solid metal beads.   *Figure 78.*

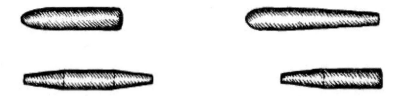

Figure 79.   *Lead weights for spinner bodies.*

on the beads, plus a clevis with a blade, and then tie either a single hook or treble hook on the tail end. The larger glass or plastic beads are best for this because they have bigger holes through which the nylon leader material can be threaded. If you want the spinner blade to revolve well above the hook, tie knots on the leader to act as stops against which the beads will rest. Fig. 80 shows different types of spinners you can make, using the nylon leader material. You can easily work out many of your own combinations.

The salt-water spinners are very similar to the fresh-water types described above. In fact, you can use many of the fresh-water spinners for salt-water fishing if you use heavier wire shafts, bigger blades, and stronger hooks.

One special kind of salt-water spinner is the "willow leaf type shown in Fig. 81. To make this spinner you will have to cut out and shape your own blades since they can be bought finished only in the smaller sizes. For salt-water fishing the willow leaf blade should be at least 2% in. long and $^5/s$ in. wide. This spinner also has an extension, either cut out from the blade itself or soldered to it, to keep it revolving at a fixed distance from the shaft. And instead of using a clevis, the blade is bent in front and a hole is drilled. Another hole is drilled in the extension arm and the wire shaft is then slipped through both holes. If you use stainless steel to make the blade you don't have to plate it, but merely polish it.

When making this spinner or any other salt-water type, use heavy wire

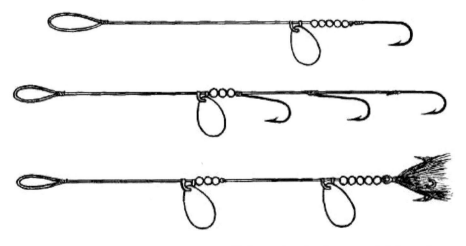

Figure 80.   *Using nylon leader material for spinners.*

for the shaft. When attaching the hook or swivel to the front and rear of the shaft, you form a permanent eye. However, if you want to change hooks or swivels you can form a locking snap or clasp-type loop as shown in Fig. 82. Full instructions for forming such a snap can be found in Chapter 12, on making leaders and connections.

The willow leaf spinner usually has a gang of two or three hooks attached behind it, baited with a whole baitfish, worms, a strip of pork rind, or squid.

Another salt-water spinner often used is the so-called "fluke" spinner shown in Fig. 83. A pair of Colorado-shaped blades are used to make this spinner, mounting them on a heavy wire shaft with big glass or plastic beads. A single long-shank Carlisle hook is attached behind the blades and this is baited with a live killifish or other salt-water minnow.

A somewhat similar spinner, which makes use of smaller Indiana type blades, is the "snapper" shown in Fig. 84. This also has a long-shanked hook, such as the Bridegport snapper pattern, attached at the rear.

The spinners described and illustrated above do not cover every type made. But they are the basic types from which you can go on and make endless combinations of your own.

Willow leaf salt-water spinner.   *Figure 81.*

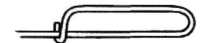

Locking snap on salt-water spinner.   *Figure 82.*

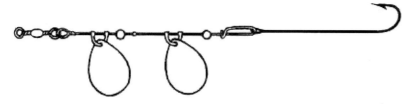

Fluke spinner.   *Figure 83.*

Snapper spinner.   *Figure 84.*

7

Jigs

One of the deadliest lures used in salt-water fishing is the jig. It is also becoming more and more popular in fresh-water fishing. This lure, which consists of a metal "head" in which a single hook is embedded also has a "body" or "skirt" of bucktail hair, feathers, nylon, plastic, or other material. The entire combination makes a small, compact lure heavy enough to cast well. Whether cast or trolled or jigged up and down near the bottom it is very attractive to almost every fish that swims. In fact, if I had to choose but a single artificial lure for salt-water fishing I'd not hesitate an instant to pick an assortment of jigs. It is also highly effective for fresh-water fishing. Obviously, the fresh- or salt-water angler who wants to catch fish should carry an assortment of jigs in his tackle box or bag.

For best results, you need a wide variety of jigs in different sizes, colors, materials, and weights. You also need many replacements for those jigs which are lost when they get caught on the bottom or are broken off by a fish. So you can save quite a bit of money and have a lot of fun making your own jigs. They are very easy once you know how, and I am surprised more fresh- and salt-water anglers don't mold their own jigs.

To make the jigs you need some kind of mold. A simple and inexpensive temporary mold can be made from several kinds of materials, the cheapest and most popular being plaster of Paris. This white powder can be bought in any paint or hardware store and is mixed with water. A 5- or 10-pound bag of the stuff costs very little and will make several molds.

Somewhat similar but a bit more expensive are "water putty" and "crack filler" which also come in powder form in containers and are mixed with water. Most hardware or paint stores carry them. Another material which can be used is "iron paste" or "iron cement," which comes in powdered form too. You also add water and this makes a heavy paste for pouring the mold. Most hardware stores carry it.

There are also many kinds of dental cements and plasters which can be used to make temporary molds. Ask your dentist to suggest one or two of these. Or you can go to a dental supply house and ask for such a cement.

The first step in making a jig mold is to obtain a pattern which can be copied. For this you can buy a finished jig in a tackle store. Then remove the hair or feather dressing and file off the hook close to the jig head.

You can also fashion your own jig by using a soft wood to carve out a pattern. In fact, almost any wood can be used to carve out a pattern, but

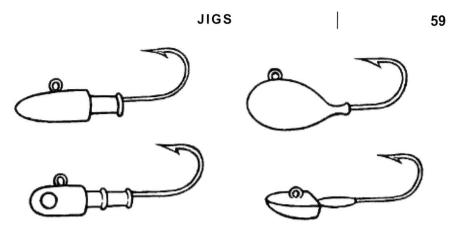

Basic jig head shapes.   *Figure 85.*

the softer woods are easier to work with. Other substances suitable for making patterns are plastic, wax, soap and modeling clay. If you use wood for a pattern, sandpaper it smooth when finished and then varnish or shellac it to waterproof it. Fig. 85 shows some basic jig heads which can be followed when making a pattern.

After you have the jig pattern you are ready to make the mold. For this you need a small container such as a cardboard box approximately 3 in. long, 2 in. wide and about *Wi* in. deep. If you can't obtain such a small box you can make one, using heavy cardboard or thin sections of wood. Cut out the four sides to form a box and place them on a flat surface such as metal or glass. Then anchor the box in place using scotch tape at the corners and sides. Modeling clay can also be used to hold the box sides to the metal or glass base. See Fig. 86.

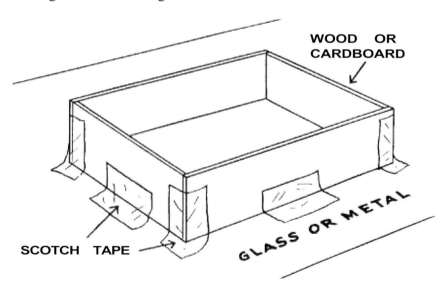

Making a box from wood or heavy cardboard.   *Figure 86.*

The next step is to coat the inside of the box and the jig pattern itself with petroleum jelly to prevent the plaster from sticking. A thin coat is all that is necessary. Now mix some of the plaster of Paris or water putty in a container with water. You can do this with a stick but your hands are much better for breaking up any lumps. Keep adding water and plaster until you get a heavy consistency—one which still pours freely, however. And be sur,e you make enough to fill the box half full.

Now pour this plaster into the small box until it is half full. Then sink your jig pattern *halfway* into the wet plaster. You should allow a space of about 3/8 in. between the rear end of the jig and the box side and 1 1/2 in. from the opposite end of the box side to the jig. See Fig. 87.

Next, sink two flat-headed nails into the wet plaster, allowing about 1/4 in. of the pointed ends to project. They can be placed diagonally opposite

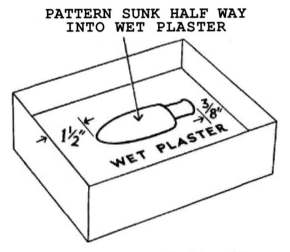

Figure 87.   *Position of jig pattern in mold box.*

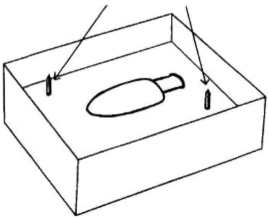

Figure 88.   *Position of nails which act as location pins.*

near the corners. They will act as locating pins when using the two mold halves when casting. See Fig. 88.

You now have half the mold completed and must wait until the plaster sets before you pour the other half. When it hardens (usually in about an hour), coat the entire surface and inside of the box with petroleum jelly or a heavy oil. After this, mix more plaster of Paris or whatever substance you are using to make the mold. Then fill the box to the top with this mixture.

After this second pouring of plaster sets, in an hour or so, you break apart the box holding the cast. Then separate the two halves of the mold with a knife blade, as shown in Fig. 89. This must be done with care in order not to break off any section of the plaster mold. You'll notice a line indicating where the two halves meet and by slowly working a knife blade between them at several points you can usually separate them with no trouble. The original pattern will be found adhering to one of the halves, and this must be worked loose very carefully. You will then have two damp plaster halves as shown in Fig. 90. Set them aside to dry and season for about two weeks.

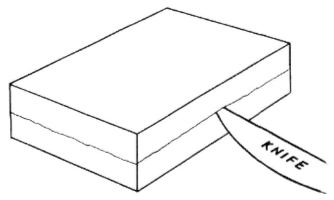

Using knife to separate halves of mold.   *Figure 89.*

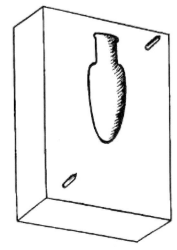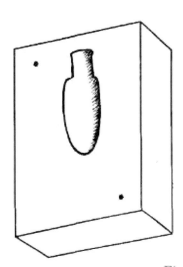

Plaster mold, separated.   *Figure 90.*

Figure 91.   *Shape of wire eye.*

This is important because if you try to pour hot metal into a damp mold it will spatter all over and will also crack the mold.

When the mold has seasoned thoroughly, cut out eyelet grooves and hook slots as well as a carving hole. First you must get samples of the hook size and wire eyelet you will use. The eyelets are easily formed from soft copper or brass wire in the shape shown in Fig. 91. When you have the sample eyelet and hook, place them in position on the plaster mold and trace around them with a pencil to indicate the part which will have to be removed. Wood carving tools are ideal for removing this plaster, to make room for the eyelet and hook, but you can also use a small, sharp knife. A larger knife can be used to carve out the funnel-shaped pouring hole. This is done to both halves of the plaster mold, as shown in Fig. 92.

For casting the jigs you will need some lead or block tin or a combination

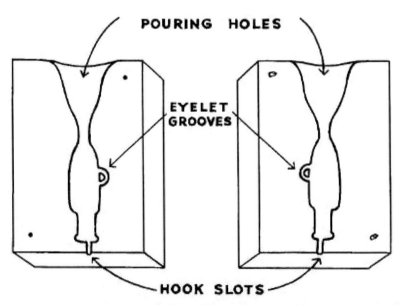

Figure 92.   *Plaster halves of mold prepared for wire eye and hook.*

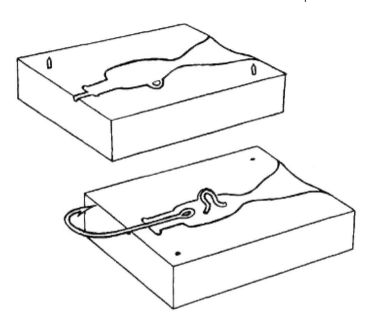

Hook and wire eye in place.   *Figure 93.*

of the two such as bar solder. Scrap lead or tin can often be bought from a junk dealer or a plumber. Solder bars are sold by plumber's supply houses or hardware stores. The greater the proportion of tin you use, the lighter the jig will be both in weight and appearance. A jig cast from almost pure tin will be very white and silvery in appearance and does not have to be painted. A jig cast from lead will be dark and will turn black later. Such jigs are heavier and are usually painted.

Melt the lead or tin in an iron ladle over a gas range or an electric stove. Before putting the two plaster mold halves together, pour some of the hot metal into each half to warm it, or place the plaster mold close to the flame or heat to make it warm. The next step is to place the wire eyelet and the hook in the groove and slot. See Fig. 93. Then put the two halves together, hold them with the pouring hole up, and pour the molten metal as quickly as possible right up to the top of the pouring hole. See Fig. 94.

When you notice the hot metal harden you can lay the mold on its side to cool off a bit. After the first jig is poured you'll usually need a glove or rag to hold the mold for subsequent pourings. It gets pretty hot and unless the plaster mold is very thick you won't be able to hold it in your bare hand. If you want, you can grip the two plaster halves together with a C-clamp and hold the clamp, to keep your hand from getting burned.

After about a minute, depending on the size of the jig, you can separate the mold and take out the jig. It should be perfectly formed with no bad spots. If it isn't perfect, the lead or tin wasn't hot enough or the mold was too cool. After a little experimenting you'll be able to tell just how hot the

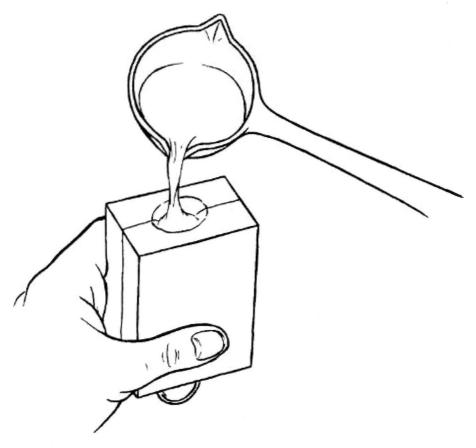

Figure 94.　　　　　　　　　*Pouring molten metal into the plaster mold.*

molten metal must be to pour right. For the best results, pour when the lead or tin has a bluish or purplish color on top. Every so often it's a good idea to scrape the scum off the surface of the lead in the ladle.

As you pour the jigs, keep cutting off the excess lead left at the pour hole with diagonal pliers and add it to the molten metal in the ladle. Once you start pouring it's best to continue until you have poured enough jigs for your needs. If you have two or three molds you can alternate between them.

You can save time by designing your mold so that it takes the special jig hook shown in Fig. 95. Then you don't have to use a separate wire eyelet and hook. The bend in the hook makes it possible to cast it in a jig so that it serves both purposes. These special jig hooks are now available from most hook manufacturers and supply houses. They come in light wire patterns which are best for fresh-water fishing, and also in heavier wire patterns such as the O'Shaughnessy which are used for salt water. Naturally, the size of hook you use will also depend on the size of the jig and the fish you are after. The small hooks are used for the light jigs and fresh-water fishing while the bigger hooks are for the heavier jigs and salt-water fishing.

Special jig hook. Figure 95.

A mold from plaster of Paris or water putty is generally good for casting about two or three dozen jigs before it breaks up. Small chips or holes in the plaster mold can be patched up with wet plaster or water putty. When doing this, make sure you wet the section of the mold to be filled before applying the liquid plaster. But if the mold breaks up too badly it's better to make a new one.

If you do a lot of fishing and need many jigs you can easily make a permanent mold which will last for years. All you do is go through the same steps in making the plaster halves. When the plaster mold is dry you carve out the groove and slot for the hook as well as the pouring hole and then send both halves to a foundry and have them copied in bronze. When you get the bronze halves back you must smooth the inside or the cavity with emery cloth. The bronze mold can be held together with a C-clamp for pouring. Or, if you have the tools, you can tap holes in both sections of the bronze mold and add a hinge and handles.

You can also buy ready-made metal molds complete with handles, in different sizes, weights, and shapes. When one takes into consideration how many thousands of jigs they will turn out over the years they are well worth the cost. In fact, it is often cheaper to buy one of these ready-made molds than to bother making your own permanent metal mold. Unless, of course, you have a special jig design you want to use. Then the best idea is to make up a few of those jigs, using a plaster mold. If they turn out O.K. you can then have a permanent mold made at a foundry. But for ordinary fishing purposes you can usually make all the jigs you need with a plaster mold.

After the jigs are poured they require some finishing. A metal mold usually pours more perfect jigs than a plaster type, but even these still require some work. Most of the excess metal can be clipped off with cutting pliers or with a knife, and a file can be used to remove the rest. Then give the jig a smooth finish by rubbing it with fine steel wool. If it is made from tin you can also buff it or polish it.

The final step is to tie on a body or skirt of bucktail hair, feathers, or nylon. Bucktail hair and feathers can usually be bought in small packages in almost any fishing tackle store, or you can send away for these materials to one of the fly-tying supply houses. Save money by buying a whole bucktail. The natural bucktail is white and brown. You can use the white hair both for fresh-and salt-water jigs, and some of the brown for fresh-water jigs.

Yellow bucktail is also popular for all kinds of fishing, and many other colors are available. You can also buy the white bucktail and dye it yourself. All-white and all-yellow jigs are the most popular both for fresh- and especially for salt-water fishing, but when tying the jigs you can blend several colors to imitate fresh-water minnows.

When tying bucktail hair around the jig head, do it in stages. The first step is to get some heavy silk, nylon, or linen thread. You can also use heavy button cord or sewing thread if you want. White is the best color to use unless you want to match the head or hair with an identical color. Cut off about a 2-foot length of this thread, wrap a few turns of the thread around the jig head where the bucktail will go, and cover this wrapping with clear quick-drying cement. Now quickly take a pinch of hair, lay it against the cement, and wrap a few turns of the thread around it. See Fig. 96. Then add another drop or two of cement, lay another pinch of hair against it, and tie a few more turns of thread around the hair. Keep doing this until you build up a thick body of hair around the hook, concealing most of it except the point and the barb. See Fig. 97. It is a good idea to make up several pinches of hair in advance and lay them on the table to be used as needed.

When you have the full amount of bucktail hair wound on the jig head, finish the job by wrapping the rest of the thread as tightly as possible over the jig. Then end it by tying a series of half-hitches. Finally, cover the thread wrapping with a heavy coat of clear quick-drying cement.

Instead of bucktail hair you can use feathers of various colors on the jig. See Fig. 97. Neck or saddle hackle feathers are best for this. Although vari-

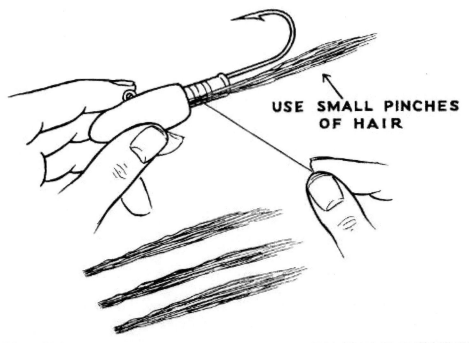

USE SMALL PINCHES
OF HAIR

Figure 96.   *Winding hair on jig head.*

ous colors of feathers are used, white and yellow are the most popular for both fresh- and salt-water fishing.

Nylon can also be used on a jig, in various colors and lengths. It comes in the natural translucent color, in different diameters and lengths, and is dyed with special nylon dyes available from supply houses. The small diameters and lengths are best for small jigs, especially those used in fresh-water fishing, and the thicker diameters and longer lengths are used for the larger salt-water jigs. When tying the nylon to the jig great care must be taken to do this as tightly as possible, because this material has a tendency to slip out from under the wrapping. For best results, try to get the "crimped" nylon which holds better than the smooth kind.

The final step in making jigs is to paint the metal head in whatever color you prefer. Of course, the jigs cast from pure tin or an alloy which is mostly tin can be left unpainted. The silvery appearance is attractive to many fishes. However, if you cast your jigs from lead you'll have to paint them since the lead turns black and unattractive. You can use lacquer, enamel, or special paints such as the celluloid enamels. If white bucktail, feathers, or nylon was used for the body you can paint the head white. If yellow was used you can paint the head yellow, and so on. Combinations of different colors can also be tried.

To finish off the jigs many anglers also paint on a pair of eyes. These are not necessary to catch fish but they do give the jigs a professional look. Paint the eyes with a small pointed brush or use the nail-dipping method described in Chapter 2 on fresh-water plugs.

Most jigs range in weight from 1/8 oz. to about 2 ozs. The smaller ones are best for fresh-water fishing and for casting with light outfits. The heavier ones are more suited for salt-water fishing, trolling, and casting with heavy fishing tackle.

Jigs are so easy and inexpensive to make that every fresh- and salt-water angler should make molds or buy molds to turn out a good supply and assortment of these lures to be prepared for the fishing season.

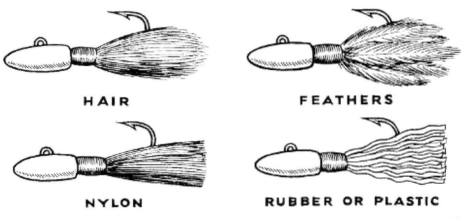

HAIR   FEATHERS

NYLON   RUBBER OR PLASTIC

Finished jigs with different skirts.   *Figure 97.*

8

Metal Squids

Metal squids are used by many salt-water fishermen and are especially popular for surf fishing. They can also be used for casting or trolling from a boat in salt water. Metal squids come in various sizes and weights, and in general look somewhat like a small boat with a V-shaped keel. Long and narrow squids are called sand-eel squids because they resemble this salt-water baitfish. Others are shorter and a bit broader, and simulate various baitfish such as spearing or silversides and other salt-water minnows. Still other metal squids are broad and deep and resemble mullet, menhaden, herring, and other deep-bodied baitfish.

You'll find plenty of metal squids for sale in the fishing tackle stores near the ocean, especially along the Atlantic Coast. You can buy one of these and make a mold of it. All you have to do, beforehand, is file off the hook and fill the hole where the line is attached with clay or wax or some other substance.

But quite a few anglers like to design their own metal squids and this can be done by carving a pattern from soft wood, plastic wax, or some similar substance. I've used balsa wood with great success. This soft wood is very easy to work and the only thing to do after you have finished the pattern is to varnish or shellac it to waterproof it and give it a smooth finish. Some of the basic types of metal squids which you can follow when making your pattern are shown in Fig. 98. The methods used in casting metal squids are quite similar to those described in the previous chapter on making jigs. There are some differences, however, so we will describe the procedure step by step.

After you have your pattern to be copied, get a small cardboard box or make one out of wood or cardboard. It should be about 5 or 6 in. long, 2 in. wide and 11/4 in. deep, but can be bigger or smaller depending on the size of the squid to be made. You'll find that the long and narrow cardboard boxes which are used to hold fishing plugs are ideal for this, but if you can't find the right type of box make a wood frame and anchor this to a plate of glass or flat piece of metal. Scotch tape and modeling clay can be used to hold the box sides together and to hold them on the base. This box or frame should be long enough and wide enough to clear the pattern or metal squid to be copied.

The next step is to coat the inside of the box or frame and the base with petroleum jelly. Then do the same thing with the pattern, leaving a thin coat of the grease so that the plaster won't stick to it. Now place the metal

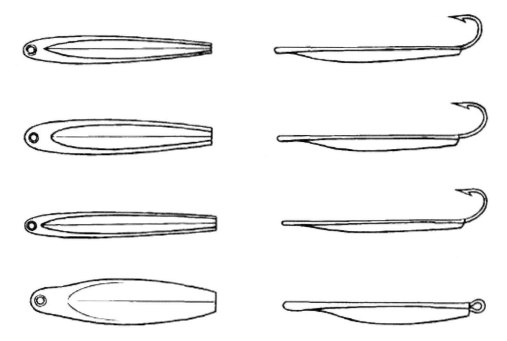

Four types of metal squids.   *Figure 98.*

METAL SQUIDS |

squid or pattern to be copied inside the box or frame with the flat part down and the keel up. Make certain that the tail end of the squid (where the hook was or will be) is only about 1/4 in. away from one end of the box or frame. See Fig. 99.

To make a temporary mold, use any of the materials such as plaster of Paris, water putty, or crack filler mentioned in the previous chapter on jigs. Mix the plaster or water putty with water and feel around with your hands to break up any lumps. This is important, or else the cast will be imperfect. Now pour the plaster into the box or frame until it covers the metal squid or pattern by at least $^3\!A$ in. If the box is only about an inch or slightly more

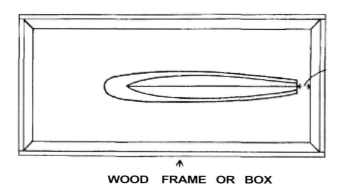

WOOD   FRAME   OR   BOX

Metal squid pattern ready to be cast.   *Figure 99.*

in depth, fill it with plaster up to the top. After pouring the plaster wait about an hour before breaking the box or frame apart. Turn the plaster cast over and remove the metal squid or pattern. This is best done with a sharp, pointed knife and prying under the pattern at the head to loosen it from the plaster. You may have to cut all around the pattern with the knife if the plaster covered the pattern to any extent. It will now take about a week or a bit longer for the plaster mold to season and dry before it can be used.

In the meantime, you can make a cover for the mold. This can be done by pouring another part in a box, with plaster or water putty, to make a flat, thick cover. You'll get somewhat better results, however, if you use a metal plate almost as wide and long as the plaster cast for a cover. It can be made of brass, copper, or other metal and be from Vs to $V*$ in. thick.

After the plaster mold is thoroughly dry, carve both a pouring hole at the head and a slot for the hook at the rear. Now take the metal plate which will be used as a cover and file a small triangular notch at one end which will fit around the hook. See Fig. 100 for an illustration of the finished plaster mold and metal plate cover.

Next you need some 6/0, 7/0, or 8/0 O'Shaughnessy hooks, depending on the size of the squid in your mold. For small squids the 6/0 or even 5/0 hooks can be used, while the larger ones will take the 7/0 or 8/0 hook. When cutting the slot in the plaster mold, make sure you use the correct size hook as a sample. It must fit snugly into this slot. See Fig. 101.

You will also need a fairly large C-clamp to hold the metal cover against the plaster mold while pouring. And it's a good idea to make a small wooden

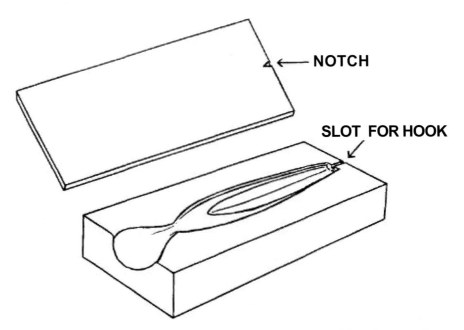

Figure 100.   *Finished plaster mold and its metal cover.*

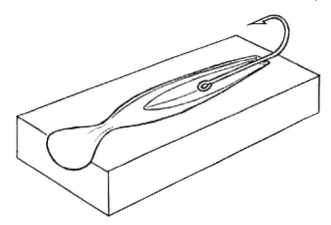

Hook Jilted into slot of mold.   *Figure 101.*

base where the mold will rest while you are setting it up and after you finish pouring the molten metal into it. This wooden base and the plaster mold
all ready for pouring are shown in Fig. 102.

Block tin with a small percentage of lead added should be used for pouring metal squids. Block tin can be obtained at times from a junk dealer
who handles scrap metals. Used alone, it has a tendency to crack easily but
adding some lead will make it more flexible and easier to bend without
cracking. Bar solder used by plumbers also contains block tin but has too
much lead, and must be mixed with pure tin to get a metal squid with a
white silvery finish.

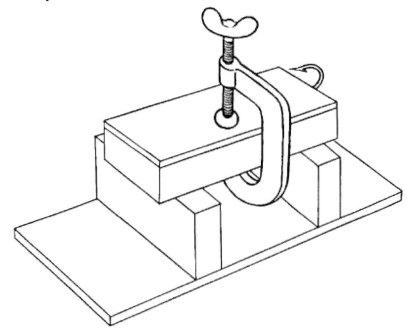

Clamped plaster mold, on wood base.   *Figure 102.*

It will be remembered that molds made from plaster of Paris or water putty have a short life and usually last just long enough to pour about two or three dozen squids. Then they chip up or crumble and a new mold must be made.

If you want to make a permanent mold for casting metal squids, do not use the plaster mold but send it to a foundry and have a bronze copy made. To save yourself work later, make sure you carve out a pouring hole in the mold before sending it to the foundry. Even so, when the bronze mold comes back from the foundry there is a lot of work to be done before it is ready to use. First you will have to file the face of the mold with a flat file so that it is level and smooth. Then file and grind the inside of the bronze mold, using small triangular and pointed files or a small electric hand-grinding tool. Smooth out all the rough surfaces and corners of the mold and then finish the job with emery cloth, starting with a coarse grade and finally with a smooth grade. After the inside of the mold is fairly smooth, polish it with crocus cloth. The idea is to get the inside of the metal mold (which forms the squid) as smooth and polished as possible. Then, when you cast a metal squid, it will come out smooth and shiny.

To get the mold ready for pouring you need a flat metal plate to use as a cover, and you must file a slot in it for the hook. This metal plate can be

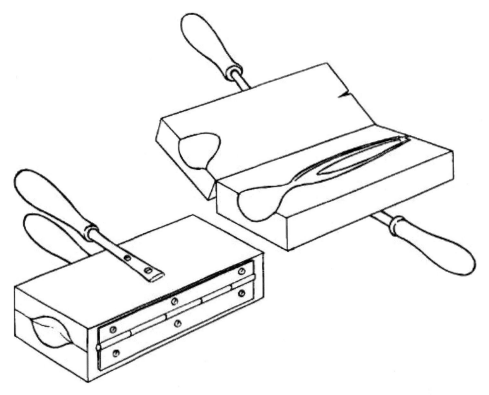

Figure 103.   *Handles and hinge on metal mold.*

about the same dimensions as the bronze mold except that it doesn't have to be as thick. You can use a C-clamp to hold the plate against the mold when pouring the hot metal. To make a mold which is easier and quicker to use, get a flat metal plate about $V2$ in. thick and the same length and width as the mold. Then tap the two sections of the mold to take screws so you can add handles and a hinge. Such a finished mold is shown in Fig. 103. However, it's more work to add the hinges and handles, so unless you plan to pour hundreds of metal squids, use one metal plate for all your molds and clamp it in place.

Metal squids are made in two ways, one type having a stationary hook which is molded right into the block tin body. The other type has a swinging hook which moves freely on an eye or escutcheon pin molded into the tail of the metal squid. These are shown in Fig. 104. Whichever method you use, allow for the hook, escutcheon pin or wire eye when cutting the slot or space in the mold or the cover so that it is held firmly in place while pouring. In other words, all the necessary parts must fit in place so that the mold can be closed snugly.

After the metal squids have been poured, they require some finishing. This can be done with a file first, then with steel wool to give the squid a

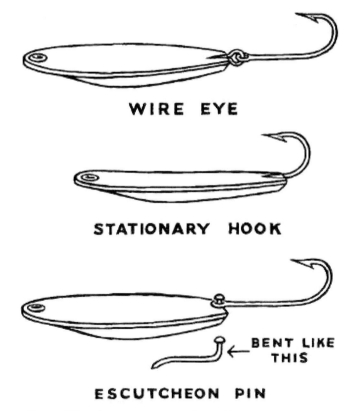

WIRE EYE

STATIONARY HOOK

BENT LIKE THIS

ESCUTCHEON PIN

Three ways of attaching hooks to a metal squid.   *Figure 104.*

1

smooth, shiny finish. The next step is to drill a hole at the front of the squid to which the fishing line is attached. This can be done with a hand drill but is easier and faster with a drill press or electric drill. Then you get some brass eyelets or grommets and slip one into the hole. The eyelet can be set in place with a large punch. To complete the job, flatten or curl the protruding edge of the eyelet to keep it in place. The eyelet strengthens the metal squid and prevents the wire leader from cutting through the block tin.

To bring out the best action in the water, a metal squid is usually bent in a single or double bend as shown in Fig. 105. The thin narrow metal squids are readily bent by hand but the broader, thicker ones have to be bent against a corner of a table or a vise.

The final step in making metal squids is to add feathers or hair at the tail or around the hook. You can, of course, use the plain metal squid to catch many fish. Or you can merely add a strip of pork rind to the hook. However, most anglers add white or yellow hackle feathers or bucktail hair to make the squid more attractive and effective. On a metal squid with a stationary hook you tie the feathers or bucktail around the tail end of the hook. Many anglers also add an additional swinging hook to the fixed one as shown in Fig. 106. To do this you merely open the eye of the hook with a starting punch, slip it on the hook, and then close it with pliers.

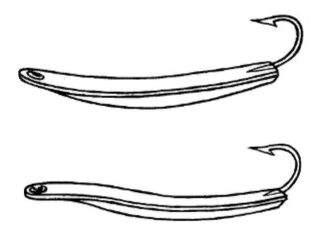

Figure 105.   *Two bends for bringing out action of metal squid.*

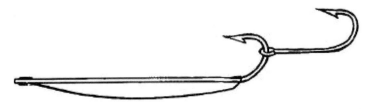

Figure 106.   *Adding second hook to metal squid.*

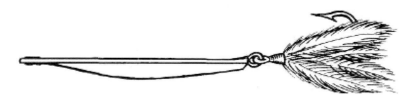

Feathers tied around hook.   *Figure 107.*

On a metal squid with a swinging hook you tie the feathers or hair around the hook itself as shown in Fig. 107. This is best done on the hook alone before it is attached to the pin or eye of the metal squid.

If you do a lot of surf fishing you'll also lose many metal squids. It pays to make up plenty of squids during the winter months or the off-season so that they are ready when the fishing is good.

Eel and Eelskin Lures

Eel and eelskin lures are not strictly artificial lures but are included in this book because they are very effective lures and many anglers would like to know how to rig and make them. Besides, they are used like artificial lures—being cast or trolled and given action in the water. Also many of these lures make use of metal parts besides the eel itself. Eel and eelskin lures are used mostly in salt water to catch such fish as striped bass, bluefish, snook, and marlin.

The most difficult part about making eel and eelskin lures will often be obtaining the eels themselves. The eel usually used is the so-called "common eel" found from Labrador to Brazil along the Atlantic Coast. The females reach a large size and live in fresh-water rivers, streams, and lakes. The males are much smaller and live in salt-water bays, sounds, and tidal creeks. These are the ones usually used for bait.

Live eels are caught with eel pots baited with dead fish, small baitfish, crushed clams, or crabs. These pots, which are similar to minnow traps, are wire cages with funnel entrances on both ends. The eels enter through the funnel holes, but once inside have trouble finding their way out. Live or frozen eels can also be purchased from many fish markets, bait dealers, and fishing tackle stores. The size will depend on the fishing tackle you use and the fish you want to catch. Small eels from 8 to 12 in. long are best with light tackle such as spinning outfits; the larger eels from 12 to 20 in. are used with heavier surf outfits and for trolling for big fish.

To rig an eel you will need a long needle such as an upholsterer's needle. It should be anywhere from 12 to 14 in. long. You can also make your own needle, using a brass or copper rod about 1/8 in. in diameter. One end should be filed to a point while the other end is given an eye or a slot to which a line can be tied. You also need some 6/0, 7/0, 8/0 or 9/0 hooks, again depending on the size of the eel. The larger the eel, the larger the hooks required. Light tackle and lines need smaller hooks than heavier fishing tackle. The O'Shaughnessy pattern of hook is usually used for rigging eels, but some anglers prefer the Siwash or salmon pattern and still others use Eagle Claw hooks. Whichever type of hook you use, it should have a ringed eye. Finally, you need some linen or nylon fishing line testing from 45 to 60 pounds.

There are many ways to rig an eel, but the method described here is one of the most popular and produces a rigged eel which stands up well. The first step is to tie about 18 inches of the heavy line to the eye of the needle, and tie one of the hooks to the other end. See Fig. 108. Next, insert the needle into the underside of the eel at the vent (the small opening about 4 or 5 in. from the end of the eel's tail) and push the needle through the eel inside of the body until it emerges from the mouth. Then pull the needle until the line also comes out of the eel's mouth. See Fig. 109. The hook shank is then buried inside the eel by pulling on the line. Now, double back the needle and push the point into the eel's mouth and force it out at the neck or about two inches from the nose. Pull the needle out through the hole the needle has made (see Fig. 110) and untie the line from the needle. This leaves a loop of line protruding from the mouth and the end of the line emerging from the eel's neck. Tie another hook to the end of this line and pull on the loop to bring the hook shank inside the eel. See Fig. 111.

The final step is to provide a bridle. Take about 4 or 5 in. of thin, flexible brass wire and run one end into the eel's mouth and out the gill opening on one side. Pull more wire out this opening, run it over the top of the eel's head, push the end through the gill opening on the opposite side of the head, force it out through the eel's mouth, and tie the two ends of wire protruding from the eel's mouth around the loop of line several times. See Fig. 112. You can also use fishing line instead of wire to make a bridle.

The eel can be used as it is with the fishing line attached to the loop protruding from its mouth. Or you can attach a barrel swivel to this loop, since the eel has a tendency to spin if reeled fast. Some anglers also tie some line around the body of the eel where the hooks emerge, to reinforce it. You can also tie some around the eel's mouth to close it tightly so no water can enter.

Instead of using fishing line or cord to rig an eel, many anglers like to use a brass chain such as the type used for windows. The chain is very strong and is preferred when there are bluefish around. These sharp-toothed fish will bite through ordinary line or cord, but the chain holds them. And, of course, chain doesn't rot or weaken like cord or line.

A rigged eel works fairly well with nothing else attached, but many saltwater fishermen also rig them with various gadgets and weights to give action, or weight for casting. One way to do this is to attach a small metal squid at the head of the eel, as shown in Fig. 113. You need a small, wide metal squid which has an eye in the middle of the body to which the line leading to the hooks is attached. Or you can drill two holes in the metal squid, tie the line to them, and rig your eel in the same manner as described above. To attach the metal squid you force the hook through the neck of the eel and out on top, then tie the line protruding from the eel's mouth to the eye on top of the squid or to the two holes—whichever the metal squid has. Finally, tie several turns of thin fishing line around the eel's head, lashing it to the metal squid.

An old-time method of adding weight to an eel is to make an eel bob as shown in Fig. 114. Here you cut off the eel's head, pull the skin back for about two inches, and cut out the meat. Then you rig the eel with one or

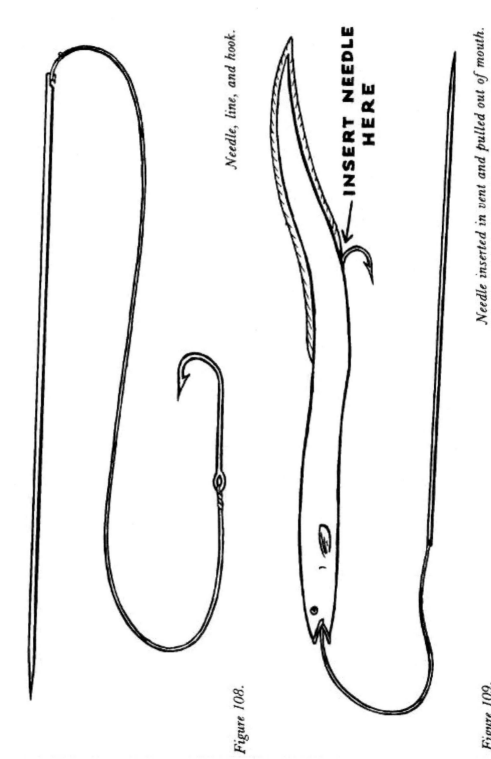

Needle, line, and hook.

Figure 108.

INSERT NEEDLE
HERE

Needle inserted in vent and pulled out of mouth.

Figure 109.

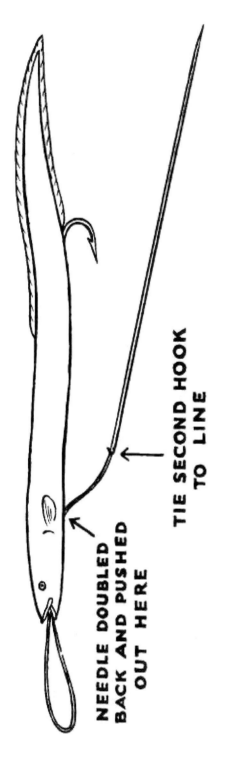

NEEDLE DOUBLED BACK AND PUSHED OUT HERE

TIE SECOND HOOK TO LINE

Figure 110.

Needle reinserted in mouth and pulled out at neck.

Figure 111.

Finished rigged eel with two hooks.

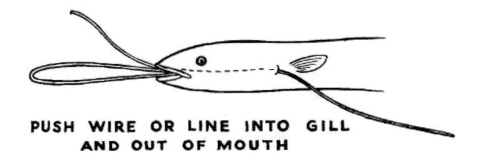

PUSH WIRE OR LINE INTO GILL AND OUT OF MOUTH

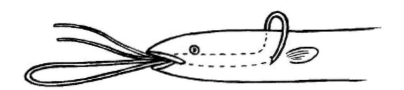

TAKE OTHER END OF WIRE AND PUSH THROUGH GILL OPENING ON OPPOSITE SIDE AND OUT OF MOUTH

TIE ENDS OF WIRE AROUND LOOP OF LINE AT EEL'S MOUTH

Figure 112.   *Tying a bridle on a rigged eel's head.*

two hooks in the regular way and insert a cylindrical lead weight into the skin. The lead weight should have a hole through the middle so that the line or chain used in rigging can be run into it and out in front. After this is done the skin of the eel is tied ahead of the lead weight, concealing it and keeping it in place. Such an eel bob can be made any length using most of the eel or just the head portion.

Another way to rig an eel and provide action and weight at the same time is to add a metal wobble plate at the head, as shown in Fig. 115. The metal plate can be made from copper tubing or pipes, the diameter depending on the weight you want and the size of the eel. A copper pipe about 5/8 in. in diameter is a good all-around size to use. You cut off about 3 in. of this pipe, then flatten half that length in a vise, bend it in the middle, and curve the upper end as shown in Fig. 116. Drill one hole near the end of the flattened section, for the fishing line, and another hole where the pipe is round, to hold

EEL AND EELSKIN LURES

the hook. Then the eel is rigged in the usual manner and the head is inserted into the hole of the wobble plate together with the hook eye in the eel's mouth. A cotter pin or bolt is then run through the hole in the pipe, through the eel's head, and through the eye of the hook. You can also tie the line leading from the body of the eel to the pin or bolt. You'll find it easier if you first pierce the eel's head with an ice pick or awl before you try to insert the pin or bolt through it. To further reinforce the eel, tie cord around the eel's neck and lash it to the shank of the hook.

Instead of using the entire eel, many salt-water anglers use just the skin to make effective lures. (You catch the eels and skin them yourself or you buy the skins already packed in jars.) The simplest type of eelskin rig is made from a copper or brass tube or pipe. See Fig. 117. The diameter of the

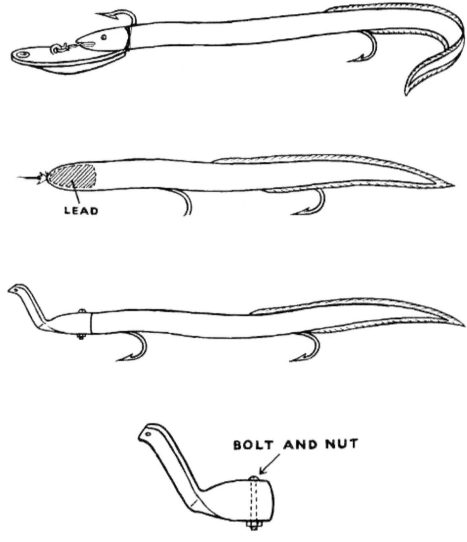

Pipe bent to form a wobble plate.   *Figure 116.*

tube or pipe will depend on the size and length of the eelskin you want. The small-diameter tubes are best for shorter skins while the larger ones are used for longer, wider eelskins. Cut off about 1 1/2 in. of the pipe and drill holes at both ends. If you use a shorter length of pipe you need only one hole, in the middle. With a triangular file, file a groove all around the pipe at one end. Now get some brass chain and attach two hooks to the chain. The length of the chain and the distance between the two hooks will depend on the length of the eelskin you use. Now get a couple of sets of bolts and nuts. The bolts should be long enough to fit through the holes drilled in the copper pipe. Start one of the bolts through the front of the pipe, slip a barrel swivel on the bolt inside the copper pipe, and complete the bolting operation. See Fig. 117 again. Then run the other bolt through the holes on the other end of the pipe. But before you complete *this* bolting operation, slip the last link of the chain on the bolt inside the pipe. The final step is to slip the eelskin over the two hooks, piercing the skin and allowing the points and barbs to protrude. Then tie the eelskin to the copper pipe with fishing line, making certain that the line rests snugly in the groove you filed.

Figure 117.   *Eelskin rig made from a pipe section.*

Another type of eelskin rig uses a weighted head similar to the heads used in making jigs. See Fig. 118. You can mold such a head in the same way as described in Chapter 7, except that, when casting a weighted head, you attach another hook to the eye of the first one, using stainless steel wire. The wire is wound through the eye of the first hook and loops beyond it for four or five inches. See Fig. 119. You don't have to attach the second hook before pouring the metal head—all you need is the wire loop to which the hook can be added later. After the head of the lure is molded, solder a ring around it so that the eelskin can be tied to it. Such metal rings can easily be made from brass or copper pipe or tubing by cutting off sections at $^1\!/_4$ in. intervals. A small pipe cutter can be used to do this very quickly. Then file a groove around the ring so that the eelskin can be lashed to it. See Fig. 120 for the details of such a ring, and how it is attached to the head.

You can also use similar rings to make an eelskin squid, as shown in Fig. 121. To make such a lure, use almost any metal squid with a swinging type hook. Smaller metal squids will, of course, require smaller rings than larger ones. The ring is slipped over the metal squid and is sweated on with a soldering iron held against the ring. You can also drop some solder where the ring lies against the metal squid. To finish the lure, slip an eelskin over the hook and the rear of the squid and tie the skin around the ring. You must

Eelskin lure. Figure 118.

Hook prepared with wire loop, ready for the eelskin lure mold. Figure 119.

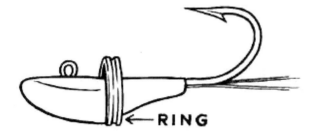

Ring soldered to the head of an eelskin lure. Figure 120.

puncture the eelskin so that the hook protrudes, as shown in the illustration.

Eelskins are also used over plugs to give them a more natural look. Here you have to remove all the hooks and slip the eelskin on, then replace the hooks. The eelskin is tied in front and at the rear with fishing line to make sure it stays in place.

Lures made with eels will last a long time if you keep them frozen or in a container filled with heavy brine. Eelskins also keep a long time in such salt brine in an air-tight glass jar or similar container. However, many anglers prefer to rig their eels or eelskin lures fresh before each fishing trip. A freshly killed eel is tough and will take more abuse and stand up longer. Eels that have kept for any length of time in salt or are frozen tend to rip and fall apart after being used for a short time.

Rigging eels or eelskin lures is often a messy job and not much of a pleasure. But they are very effective, especially when surf fishing or trolling for big striped bass. So it pays to know how to rig such lures so that you will be prepared to try fishing for the popular and much-sought striped bass.

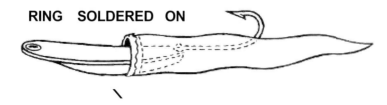

Eelskin attached to a metal squid. Figure 121.

10

Other Lures

The chapter will describe how to make other fishing lures, not covered in the previous chapters. One problem often encountered in both fresh and salt water is how to cast tiny lures such a small panfish bug, a tiny spoon, or a light jig, with heavy fishing tackle. Some of these lures may weigh only a fraction of an ounce and are too light to cast with a spinning, bait-casting, or surf spinning rod. To get around this problem and at the same time create a rig which attracts fish, anglers have made up "splasher" rigs.

A splasher rig consists of a cylindrical section of wood which has an eye on each end. The fishing line is tied to one eye and a nylon monofilament leader about 2 ft. long is tied to the other eye. On the end of this leader tie a small popping panfish bug, or a bass bug for fresh-water fishing. Or, tie a small spoon, wet fly, or light jig to the leader, for fresh- or salt-water fishing. The idea here is to use the block of wood as a weight for casting out the smaller lure trailing behind. The wood section floats and, when jerked or trolled, creates a commotion which attracts fish.

The cylindrical section of wood can be made from any round wood such as a dowel, a broomstick, or a tool handle. The diameter and length will depend on the fishing tackle you will use to cast it. The smaller diameter and shorter lengths are used for light fresh-water tackle and the thicker diameters and longer wood sections are best for the heavier salt-water outfits.

For the smaller fresh-water splashers you can use two screw eyes, one on each end for tying on the line and leader. But for the larger splashers used in salt-water fishing the through-wire construction, with eyes formed at each end, is stronger. This, of course, requires drilling a hole through the center for the wire.
\

Another lure which is widely used in trolling for blues and other fish is the so-called "bone" lure, shown in Fig. 123. Years ago these lures were made from hollow, tubular animal bones, such as those from cats, chickens, and turkeys. Today, with plastic tubes available in various diameters, lengths, and colors, very few natural bones are used.

84

To make the bone-type lure, buy white plastic tubing about ⅜ in. in diameter and cut it into lengths of about 3 or 4 in. long. Then tie a hook on a wire leader and slip the plastic tube down on the wire until it rests against the curve of the hook. Although regular-shank hooks can be used, a long-shank hook is preferred. Also, a hook with a small or needle eye is better than a hook with a big ringed eye.

This bone lure can be used "as is," but many anglers prefer to dip a short section of the head in red paint or lacquer. Plastic tubing can also be obtained in yellow, red, light blue, green and other colors. Bone lures are usually trolled "as is" for such fish as bluefish, mackerel, bonito, albacore, dolphin, and small tuna. When used for striped bass it's a good idea to add about two or three sandworms or bloodworms to the hook.

Bone or plastic lure. *Figure 123.*

Somewhat similar is the rubber lure made from a length of surgical rubber tubing. This is shown in Fig. 124. Here you cut off about a 6 in. length of the rubber tube and then slice the tail, at an angle, for a length of about 2 in. so that the side of the rubber not removed forms a tapering tail. Then get a long-shanked hook such as a Pacific Bass, in size 5/0 or 6/0, and tie a nylon monofilament leader to the hook eye. Then slide the rubber tube on the leader and down the hook. The hook should be covered by the rubber tube, allowing only the bend and point to protrude. This lure is trolled for such fish as bluefish, striped bass, bonito, and albacore and for best results should spin freely. Bending the hook shank increases the spinning action. This lure should have a good swivel attached to the end of the leader because of its spinning qualities.

The rubber-tube lure described above is trolled because it is too light to cast. But you can cast it if you add a keel sinker in front or slip a small egg-shaped sinker on the leader ahead of the rubber tube to provide weight for casting. See Fig. 125.

The rubber-tube lure in its natural amber rubber color catches fish, but it can also be painted white, silver, light blue, yellow, red, or black. The paint will chip after a while, but can be renewed every so often.

Another lure made by salt-water anglers who fish for herring or mackerel is shown in Fig. 126. It can be made from any shiny metal such as nickel, chrome-plated brass, or stainless steel. This lure should be small for herring, say about 2 in. long and 1/4 in. wide. The thickness or gauge of the metal used will depend on the weight you want. Metal about .04 in. thick is good for the size of lure suggested here. After the lure is cut out it should be pol-

Figure 124.   *Rubber tube lure.*

EGG SINKER

Figure 125.   *Rubber tube lure weighted with a sinker.*

ished and then twisted as shown in the drawing. A hole should be drilled in one end for the fishing line. If you use a single hook you can either solder it on or rivet it to the metal. If you use a small treble hook, add a split ring and attach the hook to this. This lure is jigged up and down from a boat, a pier, or other spot where there is deep water and herring present. It can also be used in fresh-water ice fishing.

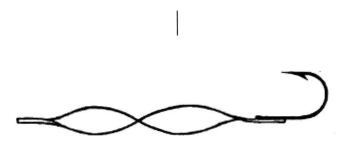

Figure 126.   *Twisted metal lure.*

Other lures for herring, shad, small bluefish, and similar fish can be quickly made with a hook and some tin foil, tinsel, or cellophane. Take a small hook such as No. 2 either in regular shank or long shank, wrap the tin foil or cellophane around it, and then tie the ends with red nylon or silk thread. Such a lure is shown in Fig. 127. If you want to, add a small feather or two at the tail of the lure.

You can also make natural looking molded-rubber lures which so closely resemble frogs, minnows, crayfish, hellgrammites, nymphs, larvae, and other natural baits that they look almost alive. To make such molded-rubber lures you use liquid rubber or latex. You need a pattern or model, and the best one you can use, of course, is the natural bait itself. Plaster of Paris or water putty can be used to make such a mold. The steps in making the mold are very similar to those used in making a metal squid described in Chapter 8. However, there are some differences so we'll again describe the procedure briefly. First, get your natural bait to be copied, such as a frog. Choose one somewhat larger than the finished size you want. Liquid rubber shrinks when it dries so you have to start with a larger cavity in the mold. Then get a piece of glass or metal and form a small box from cardboard or wood on this flat surface. Then take your frog and stuff it with absorbent cotton down its mouth, throat, and belly to fill it out. Now grease the inside of the box and the frog itself with petroleum jelly. Then lay the frog belly down in the box and mix some plaster of Paris or water putty. Pour this into the box over the frog until it is covered by at least a half inch or so. Wait an hour or two for the plaster to dry, and then break apart the box and remove the frog. You may have to cut around the frog's body to free it from the plaster.

Tin foil wrapped on a hook. *Figure 127.*

The mold should follow the contours of the frog's body pretty closely. If there are any holes or other imperfections, patch them with wet plaster. Do this when the plaster mold is still damp. After a few days the plaster mold will dry, and it is ready to use. You can use it as is by merely laying it on a flat surface and then filling the cavity with the liquid rubber or latex. Another way is to place a small flat wooden section over the plaster mold, drill a hole in the wooden flat for a small funnel and then fill the cavity with liquid rubber.

Allow the finished lure to dry for a day or so in the plaster mold, before removing. The rubber frog now needs a hook, which can be the long-shanked hump type described in Chapter 3 for the spin bugs. Slit the belly of the frog and insert the hook so that the eye protrudes on one end at the head and the bend and point are on the opposite side. Pour some liquid rubber into the slit and let it harden for a day or so. For best results, wind the shank of the hook with nylon or silk thread before inserting it in the rubber frog.

You can also use the through-wire construction, which is stronger. Here you push stainless steel wire through the frog from the mouth to the tail and form eyes on each end. The rear eye will hold a small treble hook while the front one is for tying on the line.

The rubber lures made with the single mold above will be flat on one side. If you want to, make two-section molds similar to the ones used for making jigs.

Similar molds, made from metal for casting worms, minnows, crickets, crayfish, frogs, and various insects can be obtained from supply houses. These metal molds are complete and ready to use. They last indefinitely and are very inexpensive.

The lures covered in this book will take care of most of your fresh- or salt-water fishing requirements. Of course, there are many other fishing lures which you can make. Most are similar to those already described, but some may be different. As you go along, you will make changes and improvements, and work out original ideas. Making your own lures is a fascinating pastime and life long hobby.

11

Sinkers

Fishing sinkers don't come under the heading of "lures" but since they are widely used and many anglers mold their own, they should be included in this book. Also, making sinkers is similar in many ways to molding metal squids or jigs. By the nature of their use, sinkers are lost even more often than most fishing lures so it really pays to make your own.

There are many types, such as the ball or round, bell or dipsey, bank, diamond, oval, flat, rectangular, pencil, and pyramid. These are illustrated in Fig. 128 and will give you an idea of the kinds of sinkers used in fresh- and salt-water fishing.

You don't need much equipment. A gas or electric stove is required to melt the lead or other metal, and a ladle to hold and pour the molten lead. For making sinkers, especially the larger salt-water types, a big ladle is best. You also need lead which is usually used to make sinkers. Scrap lead can

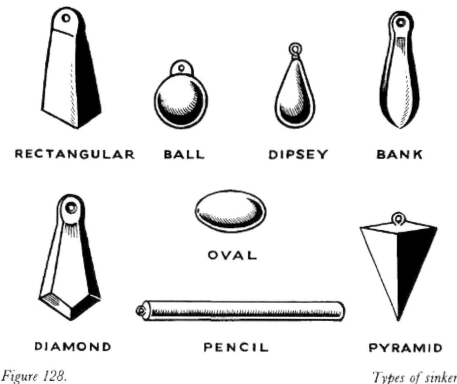

RECTANGULAR   BALL   DIPSEY   BANK

OVAL

DIAMOND   PENCIL   PYRAMID

Figure 128.   *Types of sinkers.*

usually be obtained from a junk dealer. Alloys of lead and other metals, such as type metal, can also be used to make sinkers although you usually get best results with pure lead. Finally you need a mold of some sort.

One of the easiest sinkers to make is the flat, oval type used for fresh-water fishing or light salt-water angling. For a mold, use either an old tea-spoon or tablespoon, depending on how big and heavy you want the sinker. Then melt the lead and pour it into the spoon. See Fig. 129. You control the size (and weight) of the sinker by regulating the amount of lead you pour. If the sinker sticks to the spoon, just wipe the spoon with an oily rag. After the sinkers are poured and cool, you drill or punch a hole in one end for the fishing line and the sinkers are finished. These flat sinkers hold bottom very well and do not roll in the current or tide.

Another simple and quick way to make sinkers is with a potato mold. Just take a large potato, cut it in half, and then carve out a cavity for the type of sinker you want. Since this is a one-piece mold where you use only half the potato, you are naturally limited to certain types of sinkers. You can make rectangular, dipsey, pyramid, and cylindrical or pencil-type sinkers. Although you can pour these sinkers and then drill eyes in the lead for the fishing line, it is better to cut a small slot in the extreme bottom of the cavity and put a wire eye into it. Then pour the hot lead into the cavity and when it cools pull out the finished sinker. Such a potato mold, with the position of the wire eye, is shown in Fig. 130. When you pour the first sinkers you'll find that the moist potato will sputter and sizzle. But after you pour two or three sinkers it will dry out and then you'll have no more difficulty in this regard. Naturally, the potato mold doesn't last very long and after a while it dries up and shrivels too much to be of any use. However, a potato mold is inexpensive and so simple that you can make another in a matter of minutes.

Another inexpensive and simple mold to make is to use a chunk of hard

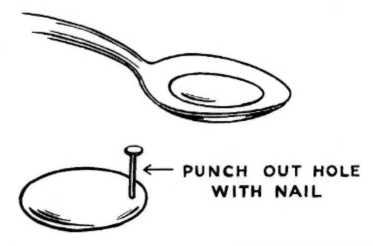

PUNCH OUT HOLE
WITH NAIL

Figure 129.   *Using a spoon to make a sinker.*

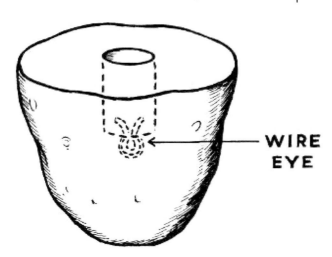

Potato mold.   *Figure 130.*

wood and drill and carve out a sinker cavity. Here, too, the mold is one piece and you are limited to the types of sinkers made with the potato mold. You can make a good dipsey sinker mold from a wood block by drilling a cavity on one end with different-size drills. First start with a large-size drill and drill only a short distance below the surface. Then use a slightly smaller drill and go a bit deeper, then a still smaller one to reach the full depth you want. After which you use a knife and gouge the ridges from the cavity. Wood carving tools are also good for this work. Cut a small slot in the far end of the cavity to take a wire eye, and the mold is ready for use. Such a mold is shown in Fig. 131. It will last for quite a while before the hot metal burns it out too much.

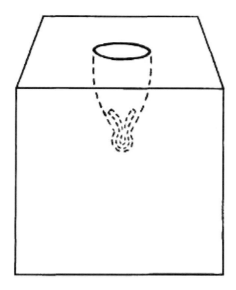

Wooden sinker mold.   *Figure 131.*

If you have a drill press or an electric drill and other metal-working tools you can make such a one-piece mold from a piece of metal. Brass, copper, or bronze are easiest to drill and cut, but you can also use iron and drill out a sinker cavity similar to the wooden mold described above. Once made, such a mold will last forever and will make thousands of sinkers.

When making molds for other types of sinkers such as the ball or bank, you make a two-piece mold similar to the types made for jigs described in Chapter 7. These can be from plaster of Paris or water putty if you want temporary, inexpensive molds. In making such a two-piece mold, you can have two cavities and pour two sinkers at a time instead of just one. See Fig. 132. So when you get a cardboard box or make a wooden frame for such a mold make sure it is big enough.

As noted, the procedures in making a plaster of Paris or water putty mold are similar to those described in Chapter 7. However, instead of using the actual sinker for a pattern you should carve such a sinker pattern from soft wood, wax, or soap. The lead sinker itself cannot be used because it is too heavy and will sink into the wet plaster when it should float in the stuff. Remember that in making a two-piece sinker mold the pattern should be

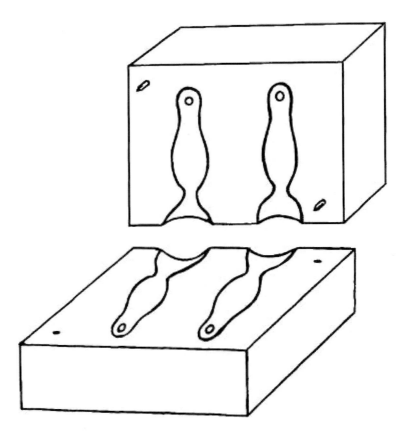

Figure 132.   *Sinker mold with two cavities.*

pushed only halfway into the wet plaster. When the first pouring hardens you grease the top and the part of the pattern still visible, and pour the other half.

You can also make two-piece plaster of Paris molds to pour various types of trolling weights, as shown in Fig. 133. These trolling weights are usually cylindrical or keel shaped and have eyes on each end, to which the fishing line or leaders are attached. When making a two-piece mold to pour such trolling weights, you must cut out grooves at both ends of the cavity to take such wire eyes or barrel swivels on each end. Such a mold for making trolling sinkers is shown in Fig. 134.

Two types of trolling weights.   *Figure 133.*

The potato, wood, and plaster molds described above will usually last long enough to make a couple of dozen or so sinkers. If you want to make a permanent mold which will last indefinitely, make a plaster mold of the type you want and take it to a foundry. If you have any special designs you want made this is certainly the best procedure. However, if you want a permanent mold for a standard-type sinker you can buy a cast iron or aluminum mold in almost any fishing tackle store. They can also be ordered by

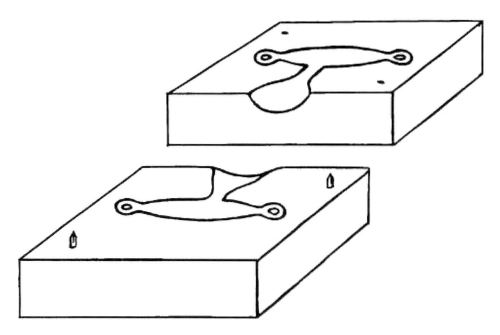

Plaster mold for a trolling weight.   *Figure 134.*

mail from some of the supply houses. Such permanent molds are inexpensive and will last for a long time.

When using metal sinker molds, a few words of advice are in order. Make sure your mold is warm and dry, and heat the lead well above the melting point before pouring it into the mold. Otherwise, the molten metal will solidify and form imperfect sinkers before it has a chance to reach all parts of the mold. After a while you'll be able to tell what the best pouring temperature is by watching the color of the molten metal. When pouring sinkers and weights, remember that it's a good idea to scoop the scum and dirt off the top of the molten lead at regular intervals so that it pours with no trouble.

12

Leaders and Connections

Leaders and connections such as snaps and swivels also cannot be considered "lures," but they are used with lures and are vital when it comes to catching fish. And most fresh- or salt-water anglers have to tie or make their own leaders. In fact, with increased fishing pressure and more fishermen on lake, river, and ocean, fish are more wary and harder to catch. To hook many of these fish you must use a leader which is not too noticeable between the fishing line and the lure, and after the fish is hooked your leader must hold him without being cut or broken during the fight. Finally, leaders are usually heavier and stronger than the main line in order to absorb shocks of casting. As a general rule, a leader should be stronger than the main fishing line in order to stand the constant rubbing and friction against the guides on the rod and the sand, rocks, and other obstructions in the water.

With the development of nylon by DuPont, a major advance was made in fishing lines and leaders. Nylon monofilament is strong and smooth, resists wear and friction, is waterproof, and is almost invisible. You can buy coils of nylon monofilament in various testing strengths from 1 pound or less up to 120 pounds or more. You'll find that for most fresh-water spinning you'll need nylon leaders testing 6, 8, or 10 pounds. When you are after larger fish you may need 12 or 15 pound test. The leader should test a few pounds more than the main fishing line. For salt-water fishing, nylon monofilament leaders testing 8, 12, 15, and 20 pounds are usually used. Surf fishing or heavy-tackle trolling may require nylon leaders testing 30, 40, or 50 pounds, or more.

The length of the nylon monofilament leader will depend on the tackle you use. Generally, it should be long enough so that when you reel in most of your line and are ready to cast again there are a few turns of the leader on your reel. In other words, the leader should run from the reel to the rod tip and beyond to the lure. When you cast, most of the shock will be absorbed by the stronger leader instead of the weaker fishing line. So, most such leaders will run from 6 ft. for the shorter, lighter spinning rods to 12 or 15 ft. for the longer, heavier spin rods and surf rods. For trolling, such long leaders are of course not needed, and you can usually use shorter ones.

To make nylon monofilament leaders you must know how to tie good, strong knots. A knot is the weakest link in your line or leader. Even a perfectly tied knot weakens a line, but a wrong or carelessly tied knot can weaken your line or leader by as much as 50 per cent or more. A good knot, properly tied, weakens the line by only 20 per cent or so.

Sailors, riggers, and fishermen use many different kinds of knots. For most fishing needs and for tying leaders, however, only a few basic knots are required, and these are shown in Fig. 135. Nylon knots have a tendency to slip if not properly tied, so care must be taken when tightening the knot. After the knot is formed it should first be pulled up slowly, and then pulled tight. After the knot is tied, do not clip the end off too short. For certain knots it is also a good idea to burn this end with a match or cigarette lighter so that the nylon fuses into a tiny ball.

Here's how to tie the four basic knots shown in Fig. 135. The *blood knot* (A), also called the barrel knot, is used to join lines or leaders. To tie it, first lap the ends of the lines or leaders. Then twist one end around the line to make three or three and a half turns. Next place the end between the strands and hold them together between your thumb and forefinger. Now wind the other end around the line for the same number of turns, in the opposite direction, and place it between the strands. Finally, pull on the two ends to draw the turns closer together. When they bunch up, pull tight on the ends making the knot as small as possible. Then clip off the ends fairly close to the knot.

The *perfection loop* knot (B) is for tying a loop on the end of your line or leader. Here you take one looping turn around the nylon and hold the lines together between your thumb and forefinger. Then take a second looping turn around the crossing. Next, take the big loop formed by this second turn, pass it through the loop on top, and pull on this big loop until the knot jams. Then clip off the end.

The *double thumb* knot (C) is another knot which can be used to tie a loop on the end of a line or leader. Here you merely double your leader for a few inches to form a loop and then form a simple overhand knot twice, as shown.

The *improved clinch* knot (D) is used for tying a leader to a hook, snap, or lure. To tie it, run about three or four inches of the end of the leader through the eye, then double it back and twist it around the leader for several turns. Next, put the end through the opening next to the eye, and, for added security, run the end through the big loop formed by the nylon. To tighten, pull on the end and slide the turns toward the eye. To finish, just clip off the end.

In order to save fishing time it pays to make up the nylon leaders in advance, tying a loop on one end and attaching a swivel and snap on the other end. Then coil the leader and put it into a separate paper, cellophane, or glassine envelope. It's a good idea to mark the strength of the leader on the envelope somewhere, so you don't get confused later on.

When fishing in fresh water for pike and muskellunge and for many saltwater fish you need a wire leader ahead of the lure to prevent these fish from biting your nylon leader. When surf fishing it's also a good idea to attach a short wire leader to all your lures such as metal squids and plugs. See Fig. 136. Then tie a swivel-snap on your line for changing the lures. Such a short wire leader can run anywhere from 6 to 10 in. in length.

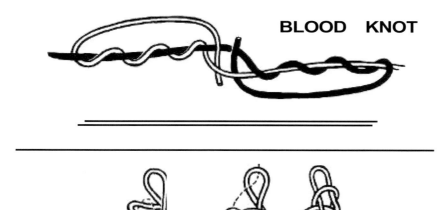

BLOOD KNOT

PERFECTION LOOP

DOUBLE THUMB KNOT

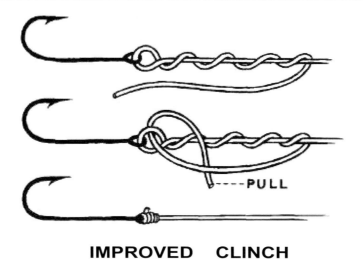

PULL

IMPROVED CLINCH

Basic leader knots.   *Figure 135.*

Figure 136.   *Short wire leader on a lure.*

Two kinds of metal leaders are usually used for fishing: the single-strand wire and cable wire. The single strand is made from either tinned piano wire or stainless steel wire. Tinned piano wire is suitable for fresh-water fishing but stainless steel wire is best for salt-water leaders. In fact, stainless steel wire is so inexpensive that it can be used for most of your metal leaders. You can buy it from the mail-order supply houses or in most fishing tackle stores, in coils of 25 feet or longer.

Stainless steel wire comes in various diameters and strengths, from No. 2 which tests about 27 pounds on up to No. 18 which tests about 325 pounds. The lower numbers are used for fresh-water fishing and light salt-water fishing; the higher numbers are used for surf fishing and big salt-water fish.

To make metal leaders from stainless steel wire you'll need diagonal cutting pliers, flat-nose pliers, and round-nosed pliers. For thinner wire, use the smaller jeweler's round-nosed pliers. For the heavier leaders the larger round-nosed pliers are required.

The whole secret in making wire leaders is learning how to form and twist the eyes on the ends properly. It's surprising how few fresh- or salt-water anglers know how to make a neat, secure eye on a wire leader. Most of the wire leaders are sloppy and often insecure. Many surf anglers and mates and captains on charter boats know how to make good wire leaders. If you can get one of these men to show you how to form and twist the wire leaders you'll soon learn how to make good leaders. By following the instructions and drawings given here, however, and with a little practice, you can learn how to make neat, secure wire leaders.

The first step when making a single-strand wire leader is to clip off a section of the stainless steel wire. When doing this, you must make allowances for the length of the wire used to form the eyes and the twists. In other words, if you want a wire leader 12 in. long with an eye on each end you will have to start with a section of wire at least 17 or 18 in. long. The longer the end you allow the easier it will be to work with. Experiment at first to see how long a piece you will need; after that, cut all the wire pieces the same length. Use diagonal pliers to cut the wire into the proper lengths.

To form the eye, grab the wire about two inches from the end with round-nosed pliers (Fig. 137A) and twist the pliers to the right to form a loop (Fig. 137B). Next, grab the end of the loop or eye with a pair of flat-nosed pliers (Fig. 137C). Hold the wire or shift it so that the short end overlaps the main wire on your side. Now, using the right thumb and index finger, hold and twist the two wires at the point where they cross to the right (away from you), as shown in Fig. 137D. Keep twisting the wire so that both of them interlock for several turns (Fig. 137E). Then make several straight twists of the wire so that it looks as in Fig. 137F. The remaining short length of wire should be at right angles to the main wire. To break it off, simply bend it sharply toward the eye, then back, then once again and it will break off

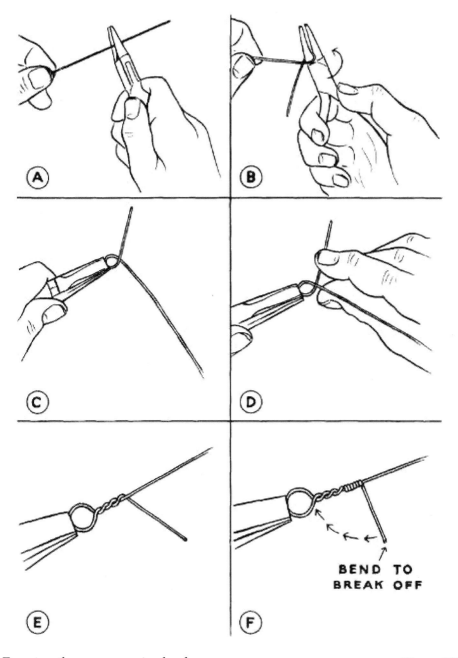

Forming the eye on a wire leader.   *Figure 137.*

clean. This is important, because if you use pliers to clip it off it will leave a short, sharp stub which will cut your fingers.

Instead of using pliers to form the eye of the wire leader you can make up a small, handy jig to do this. Just get a dowel or broomstick handle or similar round wood and cut off about three inches. Then drill a hole in one end so that you can drive in a nail. The thickness of the nail will depend on the size of the eye you want. For small eyes use a thin nail, and for the larger eyes use a thicker diameter nail. In fact, it's a good idea to make up two or three jigs of various diameter nails for making different-sized loops.

After this nail is driven into the center of the wood, take a small screw and screw it in next to this nail, about 1/16 in. away. To form an eye in a wire, simply place it between the nail and the screw and twist it. The jig and how it is used is shown in Fig. 138. Of course, the jig does only part of the job. After you remove the wire from it you complete the eye by making the twists described above.

The other kind of wire used for making leaders is the cable type, usually twisted or braided from many fine strands of stainless steel. This cable wire is very flexible and doesn't kink as readily as the single-strand wire. It comes bare or covered with nylon. To use this wire for leaders you need special crimping pliers and brass or copper sleeves, both of which are shown in Fig. 139. To make a loop or eye, slip the end of the wire through the sleeve until it protrudes about an inch and a half on the other end. Then double the end of the wire back through the sleeve to form the loop or eye. See Fig. 139. The sleeve is then pinched or crimped with the crimping pliers. When using nylon covered cable it's a good idea to remove the nylon at the point where the sleeve covers it. If you want a swivel or snap on the end of the leader, slip it on the loop or eye before you double the wire into the sleeve.

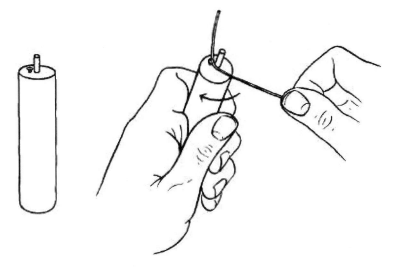

Figure 138.   *Jig for forming wire eyes, and how to use it.*

CABLE WIRE LOOP IN SLEEVE

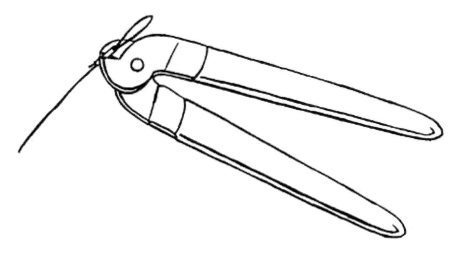

Special crimping pliers for crimping a sleeve.   *Figure 139.*

Such leader crimping kits with the pliers, sleeves, and cable wire can be ordered by mail, and can also be bought in many fishing tackle stores.

Various kinds of snaps, swivels, and other connections are often required in fresh- and salt-water fishing. Of course, you can tie nylon leaders directly to the lures, and this is most effective in clear water or when fishing for wary fish. When changing lures, however, this often takes too much time and effort, so most anglers resort to some kind of snap and swivel on the end of the leader. Such snaps and swivels can be bought in most fishing tackle stores.

You can also make your own quick-change locking snaps with little trouble, using stainless steel single-strand wire. Use the finer wire for fresh-water snaps and heavier gauges for salt-water snaps. For the fresh-water snaps use the small round-nosed pliers. Form an eye, as described in the section above on making leaders, but slip on a barrel swivel before you close this eye permanently by making about two twists. Next, grab the wire with the round-nosed pliers about a half inch or so from the eye. The actual distance will depend on the size of the snap you want. Now make a round bend at this point, turning the wire toward the eye. Next, grab the wire again with the pliers, near the eye, and make a sharp bend to force the wire back toward the twists next to the eye. Finally, take the short end of the wire with pliers and form a catch. In other words, the wire starts from the eye, runs straight for a half inch or so, curves to form a round end and runs back par-

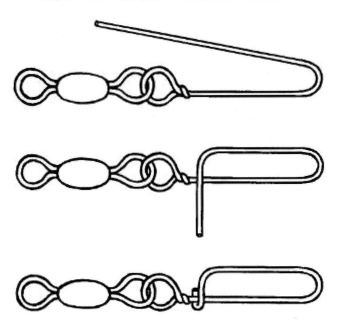

Figure 140.   *Steps informing a locking snap.*

allel, curves sharply, and meets itself. The drawings in Fig. 140 will show the various steps in forming the snap-swivels.

Snap-swivels in various sizes for fresh- or salt-water fishing can be made up in advance, say during the winter months, for the coming fishing season. They are much cheaper than those you buy in a fishing tackle store, and they are just as strong and efficient. Most important, if you lose a few of them while fishing they are easily replaced at little cost.

13

Care and Repair of Fishing Lures

After the fishing lures are made there is still the problem of taking care of and repairing them so that they are always in good condition. This requires some effort and time but is usually easy for the angler who makes his own lures. Since he made them and put them together, he also knows how to take them apart and repair them. He also has the tools and fishing lure parts necessary for such work.

Fishing lures in general do not require much care when storing them in a home or shop. The best idea is to put them into cabinet drawers or individual boxes so that they can be found easily and can be kept dry. In humid climates or near the seashore it is important not to expose the metal parts to the air; otherwise, hooks will rust and other metals will corrode. Fishing lures which have feathers or hair should be kept in air-tight containers so that moths and other insects or small animals will not get to them. This also applies to new fishing lures which haven't yet been used.

Lures which have been used require considerable care if you want to get the maximum use from them. Fresh-water fishing plugs usually require less care and repair than salt-water ones. But any plug which is chipped, cracked, or battered can quickly be made to look almost new.

Plugs which are slightly chipped can be merely touched up with a small brush, using enamels or lacquers. But if a wooden plug is badly cracked or battered, it should be given a complete paint job, using a brush and enamel or a spray gun and lacquer. If you use a brush and enamel you do not have to remove the hooks unless they are to be replaced too. First sandpaper the plug, then paint it with white enamel. Two or three coats may be necessary to cover it completely. Then add the other colors. If you use a spray gun and lacquer, remove the hooks for best results. Sandpaper the old paint if the plug is not too badly cracked. If it is badly chipped and cracked you can do a better job if you dip the plug in paint remover and then scrape off the old paint or lacquer. After this, you can proceed to spray the wooden plug body the same way as if it were a new plug just being made. When the paint job is finished, replace the old hooks or add new ones.

The hooks on a plug, especially if it is a salt-water type, should be examined closely. If they are only slightly rusted they can be cleaned with steel wool or emery cloth, then wiped with an oily rag. You can also varnish or

103

paint the hooks with black enamel or lacquer to protect them for longer periods.

If the hooks are badly rusted, however, they should be replaced with new ones. When doing this it is important to use the same size and weight as the old ones in order that the action of the plug is not changed in any way. It's always a good idea to check the points and barbs of old or new hooks to make sure they are sharp and not bent or broken. A few minutes spent with a small file or carborundum sharpening stone will pay dividends later on when a fish with a tough mouth strikes and is hooked.

Wood or cork spin bugs should be checked to see if the hair or feathers are in good shape and are not thinned out or chewed up too much. If this is the case the best idea is to remove the old hair and add new material. After the hair or feathers have been tied or glued on, the bug can be repainted with enamel or lacquer using a small brush.

Spoons and spinners should be wiped dry after using to prevent them from tarnishing or corroding. If they were used in salt water, it's a good idea to rinse them in fresh water, then wipe them dry before storing them away. You can also wipe the spoon, hooks, and connections with an oily rag to keep them in good condition. If the spoons or spinners are tarnished they can usually be polished if you rub them with a metal polish.

After spoons and spinners become badly chipped or corroded they can be replated by saving several of them and taking them to a firm which does nickel plating or chrome plating. The chrome plating is best for spoons used in salt water. If you have only one or two spoons or spinners which are badly chipped or corroded you can still use them if you paint them silver, white, or yellow.

On jigs you have to watch the hook and the hair, feather, or nylon skirts. If the hook is badly rusted and weakened the best procedure is to discard that particular jig and put it aside for melting when you pour new ones. If, however, the hook is in good condition but the hair is thinned out or shredded you can remove it and tie on new hair, feathers, or nylon. If the jig is painted it can be rubbed with steel wool or sandpaper and then repainted.

Metal squids should also be examined to see if they require work. Usually all you need do is to take some steel wool or metal polish and rub the squid to bring out the shine. If the feathers have been thinned out or if they are chewed up and broken, remove them and tie on new ones. A metal squid need not be recast unless the point or barb of the hook is broken or it is badly rusted and weak. Then you can melt it and pour new squids. Such squids usually contain some lead so do not add any more of this metal. You can, however, add some new block tin if you want to. The tin can be used over and over as often as required. That's another advantage in making your own metal squids: you don't have to use such lures if the hooks become badly rusted. Merely save them and then pour new metal squids.

Rigged eels and eelskin lures are highly perishable and must be kept frozen or in salt brine when not in use. Before being used, rigged eels and eelskin lures should be examined carefully to see that they aren't torn. Rigged eels tend to get soft after being used for any length of time. Then they start falling apart and are useless. There isn't much you can do to prevent this except to keep them in salt when not being used. Once an eel starts to fall apart you might as well discard it and use a fresh one. Of course, you can salvage the hooks or swivels, to use when rigging fresh ones. Eelskin lures are pretty durable, but when the skin gets too old it can be taken off and a new one can be tied in its place. Here, too, you should watch the hooks and wire or chain to make certain they are not weakened in any way.

The plastic-tube lures are very durable except for the hook, which will rust when used in salt water. A new hook can easily be substituted for the old one if you find that it has rusted too much. Rubber-tube lures should be examined to see if the rubber is still intact. Certain fish such as bluefish will slash the rubber tube with their sharp teeth. If the tube is badly cut it should be replaced with a new one. The hook, too, should be examined for rust.

When it comes to leaders and connections it is very important to use only the strongest. If you suspect any weakness it's a good idea to discard that leader and tie a new one. Nylon leader material is inexpensive and if any of your leaders are frayed or cut they should be thrown away. Single-strand wire leaders tend to kink, and if they have too many sharp bends which cannot be straightened out they also should be thrown away. You should also check the eyes or loops on wire leaders to make sure they haven't slipped or closed. An eye which is closed too much on a wire leader can kill the action of a lure.

In general, when examining any fishing lure you have made it's a wise policy to repair it if you are the least bit doubtful about its condition. If it cannot be repaired, throw it away after salvaging any usable parts. It doesn't pay to take chances with a fishing lure which is weak in any way. You may hook a record fish and lose it if the lure is not dependable. Many anglers who buy their fishing lures in tackle stores often use them until they fall apart, before buying new ones. But if you make your own fishing lures you can afford to use only those which are in good condition.

Index

Manufactured by Amazon.ca
Acheson, AB

14465804R00063